Sustainable Development Goals Series

The **Sustainable Development Goals Series** is Springer Nature's inaugural cross-imprint book series that addresses and supports the United Nations' seventeen Sustainable Development Goals. The series fosters comprehensive research focused on these global targets and endeavours to address some of society's greatest grand challenges. The SDGs are inherently multidisciplinary, and they bring people working across different fields together and working towards a common goal. In this spirit, the Sustainable Development Goals series is the first at Springer Nature to publish books under both the Springer and Palgrave Macmillan imprints, bringing the strengths of our imprints together.

The Sustainable Development Goals Series is organized into eighteen subseries: one subseries based around each of the seventeen respective Sustainable Development Goals, and an eighteenth subseries, "Connecting the Goals," which serves as a home for volumes addressing multiple goals or studying the SDGs as a whole. Each subseries is guided by an expert Subseries Advisor with years or decades of experience studying and addressing core components of their respective Goal.

The SDG Series has a remit as broad as the SDGs themselves, and contributions are welcome from scientists, academics, policymakers, and researchers working in fields related to any of the seventeen goals. If you are interested in contributing a monograph or curated volume to the series, please contact the Publishers: Zachary Romano [Springer; zachary.romano@springer.com] and Rachael Ballard [Palgrave Macmillan; rachael.ballard@palgrave.com].

Chukwuemeka Ezenwa Osuigwe

Leadership and Economic Development Challenges in Post-Colonial Africa

Creating Inclusive Economic Growth

palgrave
macmillan

Chukwuemeka Ezenwa Osuigwe
Director Sanemy Development Consultants
Johannesburg, South Africa

ISSN 2523-3084 ISSN 2523-3092 (electronic)
Sustainable Development Goals Series
ISBN 978-3-031-45662-6 ISBN 978-3-031-45663-3 (eBook)
https://doi.org/10.1007/978-3-031-45663-3

This Palgrave Macmillan imprint is published by the registered company Springer Nature Switzerland AG.
The registered company address is: Gewerbestrasse 11, 6330 Cham, Switzerland

This book is dedicated to those who genuinely plan and support African sustainable development. To my lovely family, the Osuigwes, my wife, Sanelisile Mbali Osuigwe and our children Ugochukwu, Amara and Aku, for their support and patience. I also dedicate this work to my late father, "Merit" Eric Chukwuemeka Osuigwe and my mother, Mrs. Idah Osuigwe. To Mr. Peter Obi for his exemplary leadership as the former Governor of Anambra State.

Foreword

The importance of good leadership has come into question when considering the numerous challenges Africa faces despite decades of independence and technological and industrial innovation growth. The problem is leadership challenges in Africa or developed countries' lack of support for Africa's development. These challenges include increased poverty, insecurities, gender disparities, corruption, illiteracy, emigration, deindustrialisation, education, post-independency pseudo-leaders, limited agricultural development, lack of youth involvement, and pitiable infrastructural development. Despite these challenges, Africa has shown resilience to development, but it does not meaningfully impact the development of Africa's sustainable social and economic growth. Limited impact on the development of Africa could be directed to poor leadership.

Given these challenges and problems, this book argues that Africa's primary challenge is leadership. The book examines the pre-colonial leaders and finds that African people will do better with the right mindset of leaders in the pre-colonial period. Acknowledging the reality of the African challenges, it highlights leadership and political elites' role in the continent's underdevelopment. The book's key features are to accept African challenges as a step towards finding solutions; the book becomes a step towards academic and professional engagement on Africa's social and economic development through exemplary leadership. The book examines the existing knowledge of the past and current state of social and economic development of some countries in Africa. Ultimately, it provided recommendations for improving leadership in Africa and enhancing Africa's sustainable development.

I am convinced that this book is a valuable resource for leaders, activists, academics, policymakers, researchers, strategy developers, students, politicians, economists, and social scientists in the needed engagement on the Leadership and Economic Development Challenges in Post-Colonial Africa—Creating Inclusive Economic Growth.

Department of Urban and Regional Planning
University of Johannesburg,
Johannesburg, South Africa

Trynos Gumbo

Preface

The visions of pre-colonial political elites for the social and economic liberation of Africa were the inspiration that led to the pursuit of self-determination and independence. It was an expectation that change in political, social, and economic leadership from the colonists would lead to the transformation of Africa's resources into assets for development, justice, and equity. There would be access to the involvement and participation of Africans in social, political, and economic development. However, over five decades after the independence of many African countries, the continent is still experiencing extreme social and economic challenges. Leadership and Economic Development Challenges in Post-Colonial Africa Creating Inclusive Economic Growth explores the reasons behind the development challenges African countries experience because of flawed leadership. The challenges include poor educational facilities and systems, insecurities, corruption, poverty, deindustrialisation, poor infrastructural development, skill migration, processing of minerals to finish goods, poor governance, lack of accountability and transparency, gender disparities, and inefficient services. It explores the pre-colonial era of inclusive political, social, and economic participation to make a comparison with the present leadership challenges.

My interest in African affairs started during my secondary school education. I was curious about African countries' geographical makeup and natural resources. For this reason, I chose geography, economics, and government studies as the subjects in my secondary school. By the time I was in universities for my honours, masters, and PhD, I had developed a keen interest in African development, mainly the reasons why the African continent is experiencing unsustainable social and economic growth despite abundant natural resources. I have continued to engage in these discussions while working in the private and public sectors. All these encounters with different professionals have shaped my views on Africa's development capacity and challenges. Discussions and engagement with various social and economic backgrounds, races, groups, arguments, literature reviews, and desktop research enrich this book.

Some linked the slow pace of development in Africa to the abusive policies of colonial governments and the selfish commercial motives of the West. At the same time, few people believe that the impact of bad leadership in many African countries is a challenge to Africa's unsustainable development. The Leadership and Economic Development Challenges in Post-Colonial Africa—Creating Inclusive Economic Growth advocates that Africans should be responsible for their destiny in harmony with the outside world rather than hanging it on the external bodies and world. Nevertheless, it should be acknowledged that the external world exists and plays a role in shaping the world.

The book adds to ongoing research and debate on corruption, conflicts, exclusion of women and youths' participation in decision-making and governance. It expresses the impact of unethical behaviours as contributors to development challenges. It explores how poor research impedes Africa's development. It highlights why Africa's natural resources and good agricultural land have not positively impacted development but led to conflicts and corruption. Issues such as labour exploitation, financial leakage, and poor education in the continent's underdevelopment are highlighted. The impact of pseudo-leadership is highlighted to express their roles on ethnicity, political alliances, nepotism, and favouritism as factors that weaken the potential for development. This book aims to reveal the inclusive growth of the pre-colonial people, create awareness of the weak leadership of post-colonial governments, and recommend possible solutions.

Johannesburg, South Africa — Chukwuemeka Ezenwa Osuigwe

Acknowledgements

Thanks to my wife, Mrs. Sanelisile Osuigwe, who assisted in editing the book while still working on her commitments. She numerously raised issues on the challenges of African development. Thank you for your love, encouragement, and support. Thank you, Prof Felix Okonta, Dr. Emeka Icheku, Mr. Tshepo Mmamaro, Mr. Solomon Selogilwe, Dr. Remy Nnadozie, Dr. Ikechukwu Achilonu, Chikadebia Anyanwu, Dr. Gamuchirai Mutezo, Dr. Cathine Ndida, Mr. Jeffrey Malatji, Mr Andre Van De Walt, Mr. Tshepo Baloyi, and all the professionals, academicians, and researchers that I engaged on the topic, for your invaluable debates and arguments around the issue were of great value; however, some of our views have to defer. In your time of need, may God find and bless you all.

I am grateful to the series editor, who provided helpful feedback and guidance on functional source materials. Reasonable efforts have been made to present the material in this book through a deeper refinement of existing literature, arguments, and debates and, more so, uncovered insights for data collection and distillation. In cases where there have been any oversights, such mistakes remain my own, and I am ready to correct them if needed.

Contents

About the Author

Dr. Chukwuemeka Ezenwa Osuigwe is the Director of Sanemy Development Consultants, specialised in Policy Development, Strategic Planning, Social Economic Development, Special Economic Zones, Local Economic Development, Upgrading of Informal Settlements, Town and Regional Planning, Integration and Research. He is the President of Mbaise Welfare Association, an NGO interested in assisting the under-privileged. Osuigwe is a strategic planner, policy developer, and activist interested in Africa's sustainable development and integration. He is also a professional town and regional planner registered with SACPLAN. Chukwuemeka Osuigwe's years of professional activities and development have a keen interest in Political Economy, Regional Planning and Development, Integration in Africa, Special Economic Zones, Local Economic Development, Spatial Economy and Planning, Sustainable Environmental Development, Borders and Cross Border and Urban Informality and Governance.

Acronyms and Abbreviations

AFDB	Africa Development Bank
AFDL	Alliance des Forces Democratiques pour la Liberation du Congo-Zaire
AG	Action Group
ANC	Africa National Congress
APC	All Progressive Congress
AU	African Union
BEI	Black Entrepreneurship Initiative
CNBC	Consumer News and Business Channel
COD	Congress of Democrats
COSAS	Congress of South African Students
COSATU	*Congress of South African Trade Unions*
CPI	Corruption Perceptions Index
DA	Democratic Alliance
DPP	Director of Public Prosecution
DRC	Democratic Republic of Congo
ECOWAS	Economic Community of West African States
EFF	Economic Freedom Fighters
FAO	Food and Agricultural Organization of the United Nations
FNCI	Forces Nouvelles de Cote d'Ivoire
FNLA	National Front for the Liberation of Angola
FPI	Front Populaire Ivoirien
GDP	Gross Domestic Product
GVC	Global Value Chain
HSRC	Human Science and Research Council
ID	Identity Card
IFP	Inkatha Freedom Party

ILO	International Labour Organisation
IPOB	Indigenous People of Biafra
ITT	International Telephone and Telegraph
IPF	Ivorian Popular Front
MASSOB	Movement for Actualization of the Sovereign State of Biafra
MDC	Movement for Democratic Change
MK	Umkhonto WeSizwe
MPLA	Movement for the Liberation of Angola
MW	Megawatts
NCNC	The National Convention of Nigerian Citizens
NCP	National Congress Party
NIF	National Islamic Front
NNPC	Nigerian National Petroleum Corporation
NPC	Nigerian People's Congress
NRA	National Resistance Army
NRF	National Redemption Front
OAU	Organization of African Union
OECD	Organisation for Economic Co-operation and Development
PAC	Pan Africanist Congress
PDP	People's Democratic Party
SADC	Southern Africa Development Community
SACPO	South Africa Coloured People Organization
SAICA	South African Institute of Chartered Accountants
SACTU	South African Congress of Trade Unions
SDG	Sustainable Development Goals
SIU	South Africa Special Investigation Unit
SMME	Small, Micro, Medium Enterprises
SPLA/M	Sudan People's Liberation Army/Movement
TWH	Terawatt per hour (TWH)
UDI	Unilateral Declaration of Independence
UN	United Nations
UNHRC	United Nations Human Rights Council
UNICEF	United Nations International Children's Emergency Fund
UNDP	United Nations Development Programme
UNIDO	United Nations Industrial Development Organization
UNITA	Union for the Total Independence of Angola
UNSC	United Nations Security Council
UPC	Uganda People's Congress
VET	Vocational Education and Training
VOA	Voice of America
WHO	World Health Organization
ZANU	Zimbabwe African National Union
ZANU_PF	The Zimbabwe African National Union-Patriotic Front
ZAPU	Zimbabwe African People's Union

List of Figures

List of Tables

CHAPTER 1

Background

1.1 Introduction

Leadership and Economic Development Challenges in Post-Colonial Africa—Creating Inclusive Economic Growth supports the idea that African challenges are squarely leadership crises. Is Africa worse than it was five decades ago? There is no direct answer to this question. Today, Africans have greater access to telecommunications, roads, electricity, water, health facilities, education, and other social and economic facilities. There are more stock markets in Africa operating successfully than three decades ago. Some African countries' bond markets are successful by turning out profits. Some countries are recording economic growth above 5% yearly. Despite all the documented development, the United Nations said, sub-Saharan Africa remains the poorest region in the world, with more than 40% of its population living on less than 2 dollars a day. Correspondingly, per capita income has depreciated rather than increased.

More towns have become deindustrialised. From the 1980s to the year 2000, poverty in Africa doubled. Politically, many countries remain undemocratic. The continent has witnessed more violent conflicts than in the early years of independence. Corruption and fraud are nightmares. Access to better infrastructure is limited. The gaps in inequalities are increasing yearly, leading to more economic trials. These travails are the product of weak leadership that needs the credentials of good leadership. Leaders who take consultation as criticism and personal attack, opposition

C. E. Osuigwe, *Leadership and Economic Development Challenges in Post-Colonial Africa*, Sustainable Development Goals Series,
https://doi.org/10.1007/978-3-031-45663-3_1

as a contest, and recommendation as a challenge to their authorities rather than as a means for a prosperous society.

Who is a leader? A leader is a person who knows how to direct resources and see to the successful implementation of the resources for the benefit of the organisation or country, someone who can identify potentials and leverage those potentials for his or her organisation or country's benefits. In the book *Long Walk to Freedom*, Mandela (1995, p. 627), one of the world's most significant leaders, said, "There are times when a leader must move out ahead of the flock, go off in a new direction, confident that he is leading his people the right way".

What is expected of a leader is to lead society to sustainable development that will create opportunities for the citizens to empower and grow socially and economically. The expectation is not a wishful dream but sizable achievement because there is no natural trouble with Africa but purely weak leadership. Achebe (1984, p. 9) said, "The trouble with Nigeria is simply and squarely a failure of leadership. There is nothing basically wrong with the Nigerian character, and there is nothing wrong with the Nigerian land, climate, water, air, or anything else. The Nigerian problem is the unwillingness or inability of its leaders to rise to the responsibility, to the challenge of personal example, which is the hallmark of true leadership". The African land and environment are fine; African challenges need leaders who do not encourage corruption, insecurity, underdevelop the education and health system or provide poor-quality infrastructure with higher budgets and disregard inclusive governance.

Amidst these challenges, leaders have shown little enthusiasm and bargaining power needed in external trade treaties, manifested in poor negotiation skills. Similarly, capitalism has not fared well in Africa because of the type witnessed on the continent that could be regarded as rental capitalism. Rental capitalism involves mining and contract/tender with little contribution to manufacturing. It has effects on the industrial development of the continent. The pre-colonial societies were engineered through the kingdom chiefs and aristocrats as a form of community capitalism. Community capitalism could be defined as capitalism that gives priorities to the communities first before individuals. It is an economic system that allows economic redistribution for community goals.

The justice system is not protected by leadership. It negatively impacts human rights and investors' confidence needed for economic development. Equally, ethnic alliance, regionalism, package politics, religious alliance, and selfish agendas affect the outcome of political systems and the continent. It is a politics that equates ideas with money rather than experience and professionalism, and it throws the voice of the youth and women to the periphery of decision-making. Finally, the book provides recommendations for addressing some of the challenges highlighted.

1.2 Insight into the African Underdevelopment

This section highlights some of the bordering issues around Africa and opens the reader to understand the book's insight. The insight examines some of the social and economic indicators that throw open Africa's enormous challenges.

1. The first ten poorest countries in the world are from Africa, which are Burundi, Central Africa Republic, Democratic Republic of the Congo (DRC), Malawi, Niger, Mozambique, Liberia, South Sudan, Comoros, and Madagascar according to GF 2019. Most of these countries have been ravaged by war due to weak leadership.
2. According to World Bank Data, the top ten of the illitrate countries in the world, nine are find in African countries and they are Sierra Leone, Somalia, Benin, Burkina Faso, Chad, Guinea, Liberia, Mali, Niger, and South Sudan (World Bank 2022).
3. Today, there are 821 million undernourished people globally, 36.4 million more than in 2016. Of these, 257 million are in Africa, of whom 237 million are in sub-Saharan Africa, according to a Key Message in the article (FAO 2018).
4. A World Bank Group report titled African Poverty Report, written by Beegle et al. (2016, p. 1), states as follows:
   - 330 million people were living below the poverty line in 2012.
   - 43% of the African population was poor in 2012. This is more than any other continent in the world.
   - The percentage of poverty is decreasing, but the number of poor people is increasing because of the increase in population.
   - Two out of five adults in Africa are illiterates, and the quality of education has depreciated.

5. Africa spends $1 billion annually on outbound medical tourism (CNBC 2027). This money could be used to develop good health facilities, infrastructures, and services in Africa.

6. Overall, 5.6 million children under age five died in 2016, nearly 15,000 daily; the risk of a child dying before the age of five is highest in Africa (76.5 per 1000 live births), about eight times higher than in Europe (9.6 per 1000 live births) (WHO 2016).
7. Africa has the second-highest number of displaced persons in the world. That figure has recently risen because of the ongoing crises in the Central African Republic, Nigeria, South Sudan, Sudan, Somalia, the Democratic Republic of the Congo (DRC), and Burundi. According to the United Nations Economic Commission for Africa, the continent hosts about 37% of the world's 19.6 million refugees and 39.1 million internally displaced people (Mohamed and Chughtai 2019).
8. 319 million sub-Saharan Africans do not have access to water, and 695 million populations do not have access to sanitation (WHO 2016).
9. Two-thirds of Africa's population does not have access to electricity, which threatens the continent's security. More than 640 million people, two-thirds of the continent's population, do not have access to electricity (Schaltuper 2018). The African Development Bank estimates that Africa's power outages sap up to 4% of its GDP growth from its economy annually.

As listed below, Africa has a big challenge in achieving the United Nations Sustainable Development Goals (SDGs).

1. End poverty in all its forms everywhere
2. Zero hunger
3. Good health and well-being
4. Quality education
5. Gender equality
6. Clean water and sanitation
7. Affordable and clean energy
8. Decent work and economic growth
9. Industry, innovation, and infrastructure
10. Reduce inequality
11. Sustainable cities and communities
12. Responsible consumption and production
13. Climate action
14. Life below water

15. Life on land
16. Peace, justice, and strong institutions
17. Partnership for goals

The SDGs Progress Report by Mo Ibrahim Foundation (2022) states the following:

1. Nine out of ten impoverished people in the world are found in Africa.
2. According to the 2020 Global Report on Food Crises, more than half of the 135 million acutely food insecure people in the world in 2019 live in Africa (73 million).
3. Africa has the most severe health workforce shortage, estimated to reach 6.1 million by 2030.
4. In sub-Saharan Africa, about 63% of people have difficulties in accessing essential water services, which can deepen inequalities.
5. About 250 million Africans in informal urban employment (excluding North Africa) are in jeopardy. This situation will likely worsen by an expected rise in living costs in some African cities.

The overall achievement is disheartening. While Africa has many challenges because of weak leadership, East Asian leaders spearhead businesses that produce a wide range of highly qualified IT specialists for American and European markets and their home industries. The technological and industrial development of India, Malaysia, and South Korea, which gained independence simultaneously as most African countries, shows how unsettled the African story is. Today, Africa imports more finished goods than any other continent, which leads to high levels of capital leakage. These challenges highlight the continent's enormous task to reinvent itself through good leaders to speed up social and economic development.

1.3 Rational Theory of Leadership: Theoretical Identification in Africa Underdevelopment with Rationality of Reasoning by Rescher

Rationality is vital in decision-making. "Rationality consists of the appropriate use of our reasons to resolve choices in the best possible way. To behave rationally is to use one's intelligence to figure out the best thing to do in the circumstances, using our brains to guide action by figuring out what is to the apparent best" (Rescher 1988, p. 3). Nevertheless, there are different schools of thought on rationality, and they agree that rationality should lead to positive results or actions. To understand the rationality of development and decision-making, one must look at the goals and impacts of decision-making based on rational thinking. The challenges of the increase in poverty, unemployment, conflicts, corruption, poor service delivery, poor infrastructural development, and many other social and economic challenges in Africa question the rationality of leadership in the continent. A rational leader should be objective in his rational deliberations that would result in positive impacts.

In the book *Shopping Leakage*, Osuigwe (2011) states that a person who figures out correctly the best rational possible thing to do in a circumstance but fails to do it strays away from the power of reason. Rationality involves the capacity of a leader to give an account of his or her action or activity; for us to use our acumen to justify what we do, that establishes its appropriateness; and telling reasons for what one does in a way that will enable people to see the point and to accept that it makes good sense. It involves doing the right thing for the right reason.

Rationality is a practical choice, which means it is verifiable and can be evaluated to yield a fundamental result. The suitable choice and evaluation lead to preference determining how rational a leader should be. Therefore, leadership rationality should involve two subjects—means and ends. The leadership rationality of "means" is information, and measures lead to efficient objectives, while leadership rationality of "ends" is not a matter of knowledge but of legitimisation of actions and results. Hence, a leader should explore factual inquiry and detailed evaluation of actions. Therefore, the choice becomes vital to leaders. A rational act or preference is for which the most robust case can be made out, everything considered (Rescher 1988, p. 112). That means validating a leader's and political elites' end calls for considering his wants and preferences. A rational leader should emphasise options and choices and have a decent sense of what is at stake, who and what is involved, to whom and to what we need to pay attention to.

Rationality explains leadership greed that fuels conflict. Desire reflects selfish competition over valuable natural resource rents, while grievance explains that relative deprivation fuels conflict. Hence, rational decisions should improvise for thinking and its impact. It uses goals and values for validation to determine the logical decision process. For instance, the presence of natural resources in many African countries is of great value.

The expectation is to utilise the value for social and economic development that will lead to sustainable growth. Why is the continent not developing sustainably? Africa has more arable land; still, agricultural development is a challenge. Africa has oil, coal, and iron ore deposits but remains the least industrialised. The rationality calls for examining pre-colonial ideas to consider comparing both phases of leaders.

CHAPTER 2

The African Pre-colonial Social, Political, and Economic Development

2.1 Pre-colonial Struggles Against European Invasion and Warfare

The invasion of Africa by Europeans did not go unchallenged. The attitude of pre-colonial tribes and communities was not to surrender their possession to foreigners and neighbours easily. This attitude led to many conflicts between the pre-colonial African leaders who sought to protect their resources and interests and the invading colonists. There are records of African kings who fought against the continent's colonisation, leading to wars and conflicts. In the Anglo-Zulu war of 1879, known as the battle of Isandlwana, 20,000 Zulu warriors defeated 1800 British army personnel despite their weapons. The Mandinka leadership led by Samory Toure directed military engagements against the French colonial forces in 1882 and 1898. Samory Toure used guerrilla warfare, scorched earth strategies and other strategies in his fight against the French colonial troops. In the Adwa battle of 1896, the Ethiopian Emperor Menelik 11 mobilised up to 100,000 Ethiopian troops that confronted the Italian forces and inflicted a heavy defeat. The Aro kingdom fought a bitter war with the British Empire known as the Anglo-Aro war from 1901 to 1902. The Aro kingdom was defeated, which led to the penetration of the British into other parts of Eastern Nigeria and the collapse of the Aro Confederacy. The uncoordinated Igbos' guerrilla warfare by Ekuemeku Movement held the

C. E. Osuigwe, *Leadership and Economic Development Challenges in Post-Colonial Africa*, Sustainable Development Goals Series,
https://doi.org/10.1007/978-3-031-45663-3_2

British forces at bay. The resistance of Jaja of Opobo in the nineteenth century to English domination of the palm oil trade is recorded. There were also struggles by women against colonial masters, such as the Aba women's riot in Nigeria in 1929 and the South African women's resistance against apartheid policies.

Unlike many other tribes in Nigeria, the Igbo communities did not have an organised unitary system but a structured democratic system. However, there were known kingdoms in Igbo land, such as the Nri kingdom, Aro kingdom, and the kingdom ruled by Obi of Onitsha. These kingdoms, unlike other kingdoms in Africa, did not have any military influence in the broader areas of Igbos land. The kingdoms were religious, businesslike, and political in nature. Nonetheless, the colonial masters succeeded in colonising the Igbo people by creating "warrant chiefs". The Igbo people were not receptive to the "warrant chiefs". The tension between the warrant chiefs and the communities led to political and economic friction in Eastern Nigeria. It seems Africa was a conquered territory, but there were challenges against the invading power before colonisation. There were resistances and challenges to destroy the status quo of the existing social and economic development that was sustainable to the environment and communities. It was in the spirit of exemplary leadership of the pre-colonial leaders that the challenges and resistance of the colonists were in the best interests of the social and economic protection of the African communities. These social and economic interests and activities are examined below.

2.2 The Socioeconomic Model of Precolonial Africa

The social and economic setting of pre-colonial leaders did not create walls between them and the members of their communities. They ensured justice and equal distribution of wealth among their citizens through accessibility to land and minerals. Individuals can gain access to a mining area and equal access to resources. The system helped to build Egyptian pyramids, the groundnut pyramids of Kano, the Benin and Yoruba arts works, the Igbo bronze, and the astronauts of Timbuktu, and there was trading between kingdoms and empires. The first Europeans who arrived in West and East Africa were the ones who indicated that, in most respects, African development was comparable to that which they knew. For example, the Benin Story written by Koutoni (2016) that captured Story of Cities cited Captain Lourenco Pinto's observation: "Great Benin, where the king resides, is larger than Lisbon; all the streets run straight and as far the eye can see. The houses are large, especially that of the king, which is richly decorated and has fine columns. The city is wealthy and industrious. It is so well governed that theft is unknown, and the people live in such security that they have no doors of their own". Sherwood (2020) cited a Dutch traveller, Olfert Dapper, who visited the city of Benin in Nigeria in the early seventeenth century, "The town seems to be very great. When you enter it, you go into a great broad street, not paved, which seems to be seven or eight times broader than the Warmoes Street in Amsterdam. The king's palace is a collection of buildings which occupy as much space as the town of Harlem, and which are enclosed with walls. They are supported by wooden pillars encased with copper, where their victories are depicted and carefully kept very clean".

Africanus (1550) gave a noticeable observation of African development in pre-colonial times. He narrated that in the early sixteenth century, many modest houses of stone and mortar were well arranged in the streets. Africans were clad in many rich garments of gold, silk, and cotton, and the women as well; also, with much gold and silver in chains and bracelets, which they wore on their legs and arms, and many jewelled earrings in their ears. There were judges, devout men, handsomely maintained by the king, who held scholars in much honour (Africanus 1550).

The pre-colonial leaders of Western Africa strove for the social and economic emancipation of its citizens through its greatness in farming, mining, and trading among kingdoms. West Africa was known for its numerous species of millet, rice, maize, groundnuts, cocoa, rubber, cotton, yam, cassava, cocoa yam, and several other food crops. The Savanna areas had a well organised agro-industry for producing millet, cotton, groundnut, and livestock crops. The famous Kano groundnut pyramids were in this area. The Nunu and Ijaws were well known for fishing and fish trading. In the hinterlands, the Argungu fishing festival shows how Africans embraced farming and its sustainability. The technique of fish preservation was through gradual smoking. The Kitara, Buganda, Kongo, Lunda, and Swahili Great Cities had great plans in the nomadic agriculture system. The Engaruka site that was excavated by Hans Reck showed complex stone-block irrigation canals and an intricate agricultural design.

The Nok people started developing iron and smelting in West Africa as early as the sixth century. In addition, the rise of the Bini kingdom, Awka community, and Yoruba kingdom was because of the development of iron smelting technology. Blacksmith was a culture to the Mande that was regarded as spiritual; people were born to practise it. West African kingdoms were known for extensive gold, salt, and copper mining, leading to a trade network between the West African kingdoms and the Northern part of Africa. Rodney (1973) noted that Bachwezi pre-eminence is allied with iron-working, the manufacture of bark-cloth, the technique of sinking well-shafts through rocks, and the construction of extensive earthwork systems used apparently both for defences and for enclosing large herds of cattle. The pre-colonial African period developed the production of cotton, which led to cloth production, for example, the blue cloth of Jenne and the unbleached cloth of Futa Djalon.

The Igbos in Southern Nigeria developed a baked bricks industry made from clay. The baked bricks were used to construct houses centuries before the colonists came to Africa. The mining of white and brown clay in the pre-colonial period was mainly used for household utensils and the building of houses. The exact time or origin of the clay mining in Igbo land is yet to be ascertained, but it could be traced to the development of Igbo architecture, pottery, and other household uses. Baked clay for building houses in the pre-colonial period was known for its strength and resistance against weather and climate. It was also perfect in insulation; it kept rooms at a stable temperature.

The pre-colonial Africans had a calendar before adopting the Gregorian calendar, for example, the Igbo calendar (*Ọ̀gụ̀àfọ̀*). The Igbo calendar has 13 months in a year (*Afor*) and is based on the lunar system. It is 7 weeks in a month (*Onwa*). Each month comprises 28 days, or 7 weeks of 4 days a week (Izu). The days are Afor, Nkwo, Eke, and Orie. The names of months and days in the Igbo calendar were dedicated to spirits (*Mmuo*) and deities (Alusi) in Igbo mythology. These spirits and deities were believed to have given Igbos knowledge and wisdom of the time. The names of days correspond to the four cardinal points: north, south, east, and west. In Igbo mythology, Afọr corresponds to the north, Nkwọ to the south, Eke to the east, and Orie to the west. In the interpretation of the cardinal point to ordinary man, Igbos came to name them as follows: ugwu (north), ndida (south), owuwa anyanwu (east), and ndida anyanwu (west).

Two significant factors played a role in creating and developing the Igbo calendar: commerce and religion. In expressing the idea of commerce in the design of the Igbo calendar, every Igbo community chose a day to host its market. Till today, this calendar is practised mainly to organise commercial activities and trading among the rural communities. The market days were part of a system to share information among communities and villages in colonial times (Table 2.1).

While four days make up a week (izu) in the Igbo calendar, as indicated in Table 2.2, these four days come in alternate cycles of "major" (Ukwu) and "minor" (Nta). Hence, an eight-day process of Afor Ukwu and Afor Nta, Orie Ukwu and Orie Nta, Nkwo Ukwu and Nkwo Nta, Eke Ukwu and Eke Nta.

The names of months that made up a calendar year and associated economic activities are:

1. **Ọnwa Mbụ:** Onwa Mbu starts in the third week of February. It is the beginning of the Igbo New Year. Making it the Igbo New Year.
2. **Ọnwa Abụo:** This month is dedicated to cleaning farmland and the expectation of rain. Early farming can take place this month.
3. **Ọnwa Ife Eke:** This month is dedicated to fasting to sacrifice for the goddess of Ala (land). The sacrifice is in anticipation of a good harvest.
4. **Ọnwa Anọ:** This month is dedicated to the planting of yam. Yam is used in the pre-colonial Igbo society as a measurement of wealth.

Table 2.1 The Igbo calendar

Number	*Month (Onwa)*	*Gregorian equivalent*
1	Onwa Mbu	February to March
2	Onwa Abuo	March to April
3	Onwa Ife Eke	April to May
4	Onwa Ano	May to June
5	Onwa Agwu	June to July
6	Onwa Ohia Njoku	July to August
7	Onwa Alom Chi	August to September
8	Onwa Ilo Mmuo	Late September
9	Onwa Ala	October
10	Onwa Okike	Early November
11	Onwa Ajala	Late November
12	Onwa Ede Ajala	Late November to December
13	Onwa Uzo Alusi	January to Early February

Source: Desktop research

Table 2.2 Igbo days and month

Eke	*Orie*	*Afor*	*Nkwo*
		1	2
3	4	5	6
7	8	9	10
11	12	13	14
15	16	17	18
19	20	21	22
23	24	25	26
27	28		

Source: Desktop research

5. **Ọnwa Agwụ:** The deity known as Alusi Agwu is worshipped this month. It is also time for the masquerade festival.
6. **Ọnwa Ahiajioku or Ifejiọkụ:** This month is dedicated to the yam deity Ahiajioku. Yam rituals are performed during this month, and new yam festivals are held to celebrate the arrival of new yams.
7. **Ọnwa Alọm Chi:** This is the month of the new yam harvest.
8. **Ọnwa Ilo Mmụọ:** A festival of *Önwa Asatọ* (*Eighth Month*) is held this month.
9. **Ọnwa Ala:** This month is dedicated to rituals for the earth goddess Ala.
10. **Ọnwa Okike:** The ritual of Okike takes place this month. What is Okike?
11. **Ọnwa Ajala: It is also a continuation of** Okike.
12. **Ọnwa Ede Ajana:** The end of Ajala Ritual.
13. **Ọnwa Ụzọ Alụsị:** This month is dedicated to make offerings to the spirit of the Alusi.

The Igbo communities and societies used natural phenomena to determine time. Time was seen and witnessed with actions of terms, for example, when the chicken returns to the roost, when the sun sets, and when the cock crows. Time was also measured with the new moon, full moon, and position of the moon. The position of the sun also determines time. My late father (Eric Chukwuemeka Osuigwe) predicted time by looking at the sun's position. My uncle's late wife predicted time by looking at her shadow. These were phenomena used for predictable actions and activities. Not only did the pre-colonial people have directions, culturally and socially, but they also developed sound political systems and governance that checkmate dictatorships, as explained below.

2.3 Pre-colonial Politics and Governance

The pre-colonial societies and communities were developing democratic principles embedded in their governance structure, for example, the Igbos. Igbo society had no absolute power over its citizens by the elders or the council. Governance was by participation and negotiation, and the Igbo nation did not have an absolute king who ruled the Igbo nation. However, there were exceptions like the Oni of Onitsha, the Eze (King) of Nri and Aro. In most Igbo societies and communities, political structures and power were initiated through the "Elders Council" or a larger group called the "Oha Na Eze" (Assemble of all the community). The Elders' Council comprised of the older people in each clan who assemble occasionally to decide the clan's or community's affairs. Community members of age become a member of Oha Na Eze and participate in decision-making, which is the highest organ of decision-making. The "Elders Forum", with the assistance of the Chief Priests of different communities, executed the functions of the judiciary system. The Oha Na Eze had their say on all matters; nobody was given preferential treatment, and no group was regarded above the other in Oha Na Eze Assembly. Every decision was taken taking into consideration the contribution of all present.

In the Igbo society, there were established institutions such as age group (still exist), freeborn, titleholders (Nze and Ozo), and Umu Ada (the first Daughters) women group. The composition and nature of these segments of the society differed from village to village. These institutions' social and economic functions are determined by the Oha Na Eze Assembly. New policies can be debated in the Elders' Forum and at the Assembly of Oha Na Eze. When an elder decides without consultation with the clan, the clan typically overrules him.

The Igbo institutions played a role in the development of the Igbo society. Decisions of age groups were byelaws, and the age group was also an instrument for enforcing rules and byelaws. They were engaged in community-based social and economic activities. The duties of the institution of Umu Ada were to ensure that the voice of women was considered in decisions. The separation of power in the political structure of the Igbos was transparent.

The decentralised authorities brought government closer to the grassroots and ensured people's participation in political administrations. It also allowed for individual respect and opinions. The decentralised authority system provides respect for the rights and views of the individual, as individuals could veto the ideas of the majority. Nevertheless, individuals were expected to respect the wishes and interests of the community by accepting consensus, as they could face various forms of community censure, including social seclusion if they failed to do so. The degree to which minority views were accommodated helped to avoid conflicts between minority and majority segments of the community. The system avoided intense social gaps between the communities and leaders. It allowed all members of the community to participate in the creation and enforcement of rules. Individuals were appointed for specific tasks based on merit, and the appointment duration was rather task-specific, often terminating with the discharge or execution of the task. Duties are usually assigned through age groups or grades for better implementation and monitoring.

In the pre-colonial Basotho kingdom, there was a chieftaincy form of government. The chieftaincy form of government is a system in which the king gives chiefs authority to exercise his power. The kingdom's chiefs and the king encouraged the participation of the commoners in economic activities and governance. The pre-colonial institutions of the Basotho kingdom were the *Pitso* (public gathering) and *Lekhotla* (court). These institutions were characterised by elevated levels of public participation and considerable freedom of speech, which is a hallmark of democracy (Machobane 1990, p. 23). Machobane (1990, p. 25) states that *pits* "ensured that people participated in the government and governance, and Moshoeshoe achieved an important traditional institution of public democracy". The Lekhotla (Court) is where many Basotho affairs were taken.

The Yoruba kingdoms had a centralised system of governance but with decentralised institutional functions. Traditional institutions controlled the kings' powers through various measures and checks and balances. There are the Oyomesi, regarded as the kingmakers; the Baale, the chiefs; and the Ogboni Society, the judiciary arm. These were mechanisms to carry out checks and balances to monitor and control dictatorship. However, despite centralised kingdoms and empires in the pre-colonial period, the kingdoms had significant autonomy at the bottom. At the grassroots level, chiefs often acted primarily as organisers who supervised a consensual decision-making process.

2.4 Africa Cultural Potentials and Challenges

People's culture includes language, thoughts, spirituality, arts, science, interaction, and social activities. Africans observe culture through their spiritual connections that express their value systems and actions through farming, the food they eat, their clothes, their music, their songs, their dancing, through Ubuntu and Nwanne, the way they celebrate life and festivals of good and bad, and how they interact with each other, socialisation, and conventions. Many societies and people see culture in different ways and in different lights. Culture is what makes a man, and it is also what moves people forward. Culture explains life and death and how they are treated. It comprises the belief systems, morals, and values of a society.

Ratcliffe (2018) cited Herodotus C. 85–425 BC that "If one were to order all mankind to choose the best set of rules in the world, each group would, after due consideration, choose its own customs; each group regards its own as being by far the best". Do Africans consider their own as the best? Since independence, little has been done to encourage cultural development and policies that modernise cultural and traditional features, ideas, and activities for the continent's benefit. Many present-day products were an act of modernisation of cultural and traditional activities, features, and concepts. To achieve such, it has to do with good leadership, a leader who has foresight and knows how to mobilise the best resources around him to better society. It involves innovative and creative leaders who see opportunities and potentials within cultural activities and features and tap them to benefit the community.

Walter Rodney explained how Western countries eroded African culture during the colonial period. However, it has been almost five decades since two-thirds of African countries gained their independence; why are the present leaders not considering culture as an aspect of development? Why are the leaders failing to do things according to people's culture? The Japanese annihilation of South Korea did not deter the Koreans from reviving their culture and traditions. The British colonisation of many Asian countries did not prevent them from reviving their cultures and traditions for the benefit of their countries. In Africa, leaders apportion blame instead of finding solutions. The energy they used in apportioning blame could be used in finding solutions through some cultural and traditional forms and activities.

Western and Asian leaders and political elites have developed some of their cultural features and ideas that led to manufacturing goods and services that dominate the world, for example, the Ireland Guinness, American Coca-Cola, McDonald's, Pepsi, beers, and other alcoholic brands. Similarly, every ethnic group in Africa has indigenous beers, wines, and gins that they drink locally. Table 2.3 shows some of the African alcohol and win, but the list is not exhaustive:

The number of indigenous African traditional beers, gins, and wines industries is significant. The traditional methods of refining these alcoholic beverages are facing marketing challenges. The idea should be how to refine and brand the beverages that will break into the regional and global value chain (GVC). Similarly, if traditional African beers, wines, and gins can be refined with good branding, the industry can employ millions across Africa and reduce the rate of unemployment and poverty in Africa. The techniques of refining indigenous African alcoholic beverages and the percentage of alcoholic contents have been questioned sometimes. These are challenges that are rectifiable if there is good leadership. It could be achieved by developing appropriate policies and regulations to ensure that brewing and branding indigenous alcohol products meet globally acceptable and healthy standards. The Amarula Beer and Cream Alcohol manufactured in South Africa are good examples of refining and branding

Table 2.3 Examples of African indigenous wine and gins

Name of the beer	*The country or region of origin*
Tombo (palm wine) in Nigeria is called Nsafufuo in Ghana; it has different names in other West African countries.	West Africa
Mgonbotho and Marula (beer)	Southern Africa
Ogogoro, kai-kai, apetesi (gin)	Nigeria
Pombe (beer)	East Africa
Dolo, Pito, Shukutu, Burukutu, and Tchakpalo (beer)	West Africa
Bouza	Ethiopia and Egypt
Merisa (beer)	Sudan and Southern Sudan
Marva	Uganda
Ubuki	Rwanda
Talla (wine), Korefe, Shamit, tej, and Arik (beers)	Ethiopia
Maujek and Chang'aa (beer)	Kenya
Mowa (beer)	Malawi
Apheteshie (gin)	Ghana

Source: Desktop research

indigenous alcohol. Where some entrepreneurs have taken the risk to refine some of these beers, gin, wine, or whiskies, support from the governments could be better.

One of the roles of government is to encourage entrepreneurs and create an enabling environment for business growth through policies and strategies. In every corner of Africa, Western alcoholic beverages have taken over the market. There is no problem with Western beverages in Africa, but there must be healthy competition between foreign and local alcoholic beverages.

The indigenous African textile industry is not exempted from these challenges. In the 1970s and 1980s, Nigeria, for instance, had more than 60 well-established textile mills that focused on producing indigenous West African textiles. As of 2007, the country could not boast up to six textile mills. Traditional production of textiles has been a century-old industry in Nigeria and West Africa. However, it was in the 1950s that it took root and received a boost with the establishment of the Kaduna Textile Mills in 1956, United Nigeria Textiles in 1962, and others such as Enpee, Aswani, and Asaba. From 1985 till 2010, Kaduna and Enpee were closed along with at least 70 other textile mills, losing jobs and economic opportunities. Nuruddeen M. (2010) reports that Ghana, one of the West African countries with a vivacious textile industry, is slowly joining the league of other countries in West Africa with collapsed textile and garment manufacturing sub-sector. His report indicated that of over 40 textile firms that employed more than 25,000 people in the last three decades, the country now has only four textile factories employing less than 4000 Ghanaians. According to Nuruddeen M (2010), Ghana lost about 300 billion Ghanaian Cedis in potential revenue. The textile industry is crucial for economic growth because of its capacity to provide many jobs/employment and grow the economy. The situation of indigenous textile industries in Ghana and Nigeria is common in many other African countries.

In Lesotho, Asian textile companies take advantage of weak leadership and abuse their employees by paying low remuneration. Between 2002 and 2013 in Lesotho, many Asian textile companies paid their workers a mere 120 Dollars per month while they worked 11 hours from 7 a.m. to 6 p.m. At the same time, these Asian textile companies enjoyed government tax rebates for some years. Understandably, these companies are creating jobs; however, it is sad that these companies abused their workers through long working hours with meagre remuneration while getting tax rebates from the government. Good leadership is needed, where leaders protect their citizens from exploitation by local and foreign companies.

Similarly, to develop indigenous products, there is a need for support through social ideologies, social ideologies expressed by Ubuntu and Nwanne philosophy. These ideologies epitomised support during the pre-colonial era for the economic emancipation of communities and individuals. These ideologies are explained below.

2.5 Africa's Ideology and Principle for Development (Ubuntu, Nwanne, and Ofo na Ogu)

"Ubuntu" and "Nwanne" are African ideologies that express humanity and are widely practised in Africa. Ubuntu and Nwanne are expressed through spirituality, support for one another, welfare, public participation, and consensus in decision-making. Ubuntu is articulated in the Zulu word "Umuntu ngumuntu ngabantu" (a person is a person through other people), and Nwanne is expressed in the Igbo word "Igwe bu ike" (unity is strength). It also acknowledges the rights and responsibilities of every citizen in promoting individual and social well-being. It accentuates leadership inspiration for individuals' support for social and economic empowerment of one another and for the benefit of the community's development.

In Igbo society, "Nwanne" has different expressions. The Nwanne ideology could mean "Nwanne di na mba" (there is one's sibling in a foreign land). It is a title given to a person who supports others or people economically who are not blood-related to him or her or not from the same community or area. The name Nwanne di na mba conveys the need for individuals to be one another's keepers regardless of their origins. This ideology explains that someone's brothers are not only those from his town or community.

Nwanne ideology is also expressed in the Igbo idiom, Egbe bere, Ugo bere, nke si ibe ya ebere, nku kwakwa ya, mob u ya shiya ebe oga ebe (When a hawk perches on a tree and eagles perch on the same tree if any does not want other to perch, let its wings break or let it show him where it should perch). In this case you are forced to except to live with others in harmony. Nwanne ideology is also expressed in this proverb: "iberi, ma mbiri" (live and let live). It interprets the ideas of support and living in unity. It highlights that people in pre-colonial times wished for unity in pursuing their economic and social development by supporting each other.

"Ubuntu" and "Nwanne" include concepts of inclusivity, unity, and sharing in other peoples' good and pains and finding solutions to that pain with the help of others. "Nwanne" and "Ubuntu" define each person as belonging to a larger group or collective of groups. It promotes social and economic unity and awareness of other people's matters. The ideologies support the idea that I am successful because other people helped me. Niekerk (2013, p. 1) quoted Desmond Tutu, "'Hey, he or she has Ubuntu.' This means they are generous, hospitable, friendly, caring, and compassionate. They share what they have. It also means my humanity is caught up, is inextricably bound up, in theirs. We belong in a bundle of life. We say, 'a person is a person through other people.' It is not 'I think. Therefore, I am.' It says instead: 'I am human because I belong.' I participate, and I share. A person with ubuntu is open and available to others, affirming of others, does not feel threatened that others are able and good, for he or she has the proper self-assurance that comes from knowing that he or she belongs in a greater whole, and is diminished when others are humiliated or diminished when others are tortured or oppressed, or treated as if they were less than who they are".

Nelson Mandela once expressed Ubuntu as a traveller going through a country who would stop at a village and did not have to ask for food or water, and once he stopped, the people gave him food and entertained him. Ubuntu does not mean that people should not enrich themselves. The question, therefore, is: Are you going to do so to enable the community around you to improve? Nelson Mandela queried. "Ubuntu" was not about self-enrichment but the richness of the community. It means a person must enrich himself or herself, but the riches must help the community and contribute to the good of humanity. "Ubuntu and Nwanne" do not accept the oppression of others just because the oppressor has wealth or status.

The concept of "Nwanne" and "Ubuntu" is spread all over Africa as each ethnic group has an ideology to help one another. They espouse the logic that what affects my fellow human being affects me, and when he is happy and blissful, I am also pleased and blissful. When things get healthy for one another, it will be glowing for me. When the other is rich, I will not undergo pain. These things cemented relationships among Africans for their own economic and social well-being, including the security of their communities in the pre-colonial era. The idea of "Ubuntu" and

"Nwanne" means the ability to accommodate others materially, mentally, socially, and economically. They encourage the development of the communities and regions. They involve assistance in building other peoples' futures. Presently, the leaders give little regard to "Ubuntu and Nwanne". It has manifested in poor governance. It has also led to the development of poor policies due to a lack of public participation and consultations.

In Zimbabwe, "Nwanne" and "Ubuntu" go by the name "Unhu"; in Rwanda, it is regarded as Kinyarwanda. Kinyarwanda means human generosity. In Kenya, the "Harambee" is a Kenyan tradition for self-help events and community development. "Harambee" means drawing or pulling people together. In East African countries, "Ujamaa", a Swahili word, means extended relatives and family coming together to develop others. "Ujamaa" and "Harambee" mean support, teamwork and collectively for individual existence. One of South Africa's ideologies is "Batho Pele" (meaning people first). In delivering our responsibilities in the public or private sector, if we can recognise that it is people first, Africa will be a great continent. The whole idea of Ubuntu and Nwanne is expressed in Batho Pele, Ujamaa, and Harambee.

As described above, the ideologies of "Nwanne" and "Ubuntu" are fast eluding the continent. Disregarding these ideologies by individuals, elites, and leaders is negatively impacting Africa's development. Limitations on Ubuntu and Nwanne ideologies lead to individual wealth accumulation without commitment to social well-being. This is killing humanity and humility, destroying politics and sustainable economic development.

If the Ubuntu and Nwanne ideologies and values were adhered to in the public and private sectors, corruption and mismanagement of public funds could have been minimised. Many African cities could have become some of the great cities in industrial development, regional blocks could have integrated socially and economically for common goals, and conflicts at national and regional levels could have been reduced. Caring for others and the development of others, which facilitate the development of the economy, could have been enhanced through public and private sector support.

Where there were disagreements, the disagreements were part of the process of building consensus in decision-making for the general interest of the citizens. With these ideologies disregarded in the development of Africa by the leadership, what social and economic strategies are the leaders following? The Nwanne philosophy also invokes the doctrine of "Ofo na Ogu", which is explained below.

2.5.1 *The Igbo's "Ofo na Ogu"*

The spirituality of Nwanne is anchored on the truth of the principles of "Ofo na Ogu", which means keep your hand clean and the gods will justify you; don't cheat others so that gods will be by your side; render justice fairly so that gods will be there to protect you and justice will be rendered to you fairly; say the truth without fear and favour, to maintain your relationship with others and gods; and be fair in the distribution of resources no matter how small it is so that the gods will guide you and give you the share of your blessings and destiny.

"Ofo na Ogu" expresses the need for sincerity and integrity in performing one's duties. It is composed of truth, ethics, and justice. With sincerity, ethics, and justice, a person can directly link with gods for protection and wisdom in discharging duties. That's what the Igbos call "Igba Ndu" (individual covenant with the gods and his fellow human being). The disregard for the ideologies of "Ubuntu", Nwanne, and "Ofo na Ogu" are impacting the morals and values and are affecting the continent's development. The fast decline of these ideologies and principles in the African way of life leads to high corruption, conflicts, and many other social ills that affect Africa socially and economically.

2.6 Religion

African religion was a vital force that encouraged social and economic development in the pre-colonial times. Some people believe that contact with Europe disorganised African religion and is the reason for African development challenges. This argument might have a form of truth, but compared to other countries colonised in Asia, it holds no truth, for example, the recovery of Asian cultures even though they were colonised like African countries. Many Asian countries practise the kind of religion they are used to and hold their culture in the highest esteem. Therefore, contact with the West was not the main issue with some of the economic challenges the continent is facing presently. It is remarkable how Asians recycled their cultures and religions after their independence, while Africans could not. Even in former British colonies where indirect rule was an instrument for governance during the colonial era, culture and traditional religions are fast phasing out.

The evidence is that the Middle East conquerors and colonisers shaped the religious activities in Africa, when the Europeans and the Middle

Easterners came to Africa with the bible, Koran, and their culture. They taught Africans to change their names, how they should dress, and about their food and languages among others. Africans absorbed European and Middle Eastern cultures to create a deal that accepted European and Middle Eastern religions. The same scenario happened in Asia, but Asians did not absorb their religion and culture. Ironically, while Asians are proud of their heritage and culture, many Africans take little pride in their heritage, which has affected the continent's dignity and development.

Before Europeans brought Christianity to Africa, Arabs had brought Islam into North, Central, and West Africa. Islam wiped away most of the culture of the regions where they conquered, such as the north of West Africa. Today, many countries, regions, and states in these areas have Sharia courts and European-style courts but no customary courts. Hence, Africa's Western and Eastern worlds have shaped our lives like theirs. We have lost many identities that took us through the pre-colonial era.

Today, it is ironic that many Africans from Nigeria, Ghana, and Kenya are exporting Christianity back to Europe while there needs to be more exportation of technology. Mockingly, despite our exploits in religion, there is little love among us, as many are divided along ethnic and religious lines. It is expected that an increase in churches and mosques could have sprung higher morals and values in Africa, but the situation is the opposite. Many Africans have become religious instead of godly. Africa needs people with the spirit of godliness rather than religion, as in precolonial times.

The revolutionary spirits of Africans are being quenched by the practices of many new religions. When faith destroys the basis of human development, it must be questioned. Faith works with vision, and faith helps shape the mind to believe it can do and inspires vision. Faith is achievable in an economy where leaders and political elites are truthful in delivering economic opportunities. No person will deliberately put his hand into a fire and expect God to do a miracle and rescue him/her with faith. Only in Africa is God expected to do miracles, while evil is purposefully done and engineered by leaders and elites.

In pre-colonial Africa, the religious system was one of the ways in which the leadership mobilised people and implemented/enforced social and economic justice. The life of Africans before the arrival of Europeans and Middle Easterners revolved around their religion and human development that led to social and economic development. It is a surprise at the arrogance of Europeans in thinking that they know better than Africans in their culture and beliefs. Achebe's (1958) book *Things Fall Apart* (1958, pp. 125–126) highlights the dilemma of disregard for African religion.

> Does the white man understand our customs about land? How can he when he does not even speak our tongue? But he says our customs are wrong, and our brothers who have taken up his religion also say our customs are bad. How can we fight when our own brothers have turned against us? The white man is very clever. He came quietly and peaceably with his religion. We were amused at his foolishness and allowed him to stay. He has won over our brothers, and our clan can no longer act like one. He has put a knife on the things that held us together, and we have fallen apart.

The deceit of the colonisers led to the failure of the clan. The deception also led to the tragedy of Okonwko (*Things Fall Apart*). The clan failed to act like one, just like the continent has not unified and integrated for social and economic development. Even though Achebe blamed the white man for his disregard for the religion and love of the community, he showed distrust towards the members of the clan's reaction to the presence of the white man and their religion. Many of the post-colonial leaders and political elites in Africa are like the clan leaders to whom Achebe showed distrust and criticism because of the disrespect for things that are African. They are the ones who are continually striking deadly knives into the values, culture, and morals that hold Africa together. They mimic the same pattern of forceful proselytising by the European missionaries that led to the tragic world of Okonkwo.

CHAPTER 3

Post-independence Politics in Africa

3.1 Independence of African Countries

Independence means sovereignty, not absolute power to leaders and political elites, but power to the people. Freedom is subverted in Africa because of the dictatorial tendencies of political leaders. It was subverted because many of the continent's leaders wanted to grab power for the sake of having authority rather than for the interest of good leadership. To understand the level the continent has fallen behind, it is crucial to illustrate the year African countries became independent, as shown in Table 3.1.

Liberia was the earliest country to be liberated, and the latest was Namibia and South Africa. Liberia and Ethiopia were independent well before India, Malaysia, and South Korea. Liberia's independence is over 100 years older than India, Malaysia, and South Korea, and Ethiopia's is over 50 years older than India, Malaysia, and South Korea. However, technologically, Liberia and Ethiopia are more than 100 years behind India, Malaysia, and South Korea. The table below shows some countries that gained independence at the same time as African countries but have developed or developed faster than African countries.

From Table 3.2, it is recognised that most African countries gained their independence in the 1960s. As of 2023, these countries have been independent for 63 years. Is there independence in Africa, where more than 40% live in poverty? According to the Africa Development Bank

C. E. Osuigwe, *Leadership and Economic Development Challenges in Post-Colonial Africa*, Sustainable Development Goals Series,
https://doi.org/10.1007/978-3-031-45663-3_3

Table 3.1 African countries independence year and age in 2023

African countries	*Year of independence*	*Age*
Liberia	1847–2023	**176 years**
Ethiopia	1896–2023	**127 years**
Egypt	1951–2023	**72 years**
Sudan, Tunisia, Morocco	1956–2023	**67 years**
Ghana	1957–2023	**66 years**
Guinea	1958–2023	**65 years**
Chad, Benin, Nigeria, Ivory Coast, Madagascar, Central Africa Republic, Mali, Niger, Senegal, Burkina Faso, Mauritania, Togo, Zaire, Somalia, Congo, Gabon, Cameroon	1960–2023	**63 years**
Sierra Leone	1961–2023	**62 years**
Algeria, Burundi, Rwanda, Uganda	1962–2023	**61 years**
Kenya, Tanzania	1963–2023	**60 years**
Malawi, Zambia	1964–2023	**59 years**
Gambia	1965–2023	**58 years**
Botswana, Lesotho	1966–2023	**57 years**
Equatorial Guinea, Mauritius, Swaziland	1968–2023	**55 years**
Guinea-Bissau, Libya	1969–2023	**54 years**
Angola, Cape Verde, Comoros, Mozambique, São Tomé	1975–2023	**48 years**
Seychelles	1976–2023	**47 years**
Djibouti	1977–2023	**46 years**
Zimbabwe	1980–2023	**43 years**
Namibia	1990–2023	**33 years**

Source: Author 2023

Group, 31% of unemployed youths need access to water, sanitation, and electricity, and there are many uneducated Africans, and many dropped out of primary school. Independence comes with the ability of an individual to explore economic potentials created through leadership vision. It did not take South Korea, Singapore, Malaysia, and India more than 40 years after independence to become technologically developed—manufacturing their own cars, cell phones, televisions, and many other things. No African country can claim technological development since independence like South Korea, India, Malaysia and even Vietnam, which fought a war between 1954 and 1975. Thus, more indication of indigenous technological and industrial development needs to be done. The fact is that some African countries are deindustrialising under the watchful eyes of many preying leaders and political elites.

Table 3.2 Independence of some Asian countries

Countries for comparison	*Year of independence*	*Age in 2022*
South Korea and Indonesia	1945	77 years
India	1947	75 years
Israel	1948	74 years
Malaysia	1957	65 years
Singapore	1965	57 years

Source: Author 2023

Think of this: South Korea was invaded by Japan in 1910 and liberated during World War 2. Japan ruled Korea, destroyed the local culture, and desecrated their country's sacred shrines. The Japanese banned the Korean language and barred Koreans from universities. During this period, Japan shipped young Korean men to Japan to provide forced labour in mines and factories. Some Koreans were conscripted to serve in the Japan Imperial Army. The ordeal of Koreans did not end after the liberation of Korea; the country went into a bloody civil war that saw the country split into North and South Korea. The history of South Korea could have given its leaders an excuse for failure. It could have been an excuse to be a backward country for consumers of imported goods from other countries. The South Koreans could have allowed the country to remain in poverty, citing the period of Japanese occupation and oppression as an excuse for its underdevelopment while at the same time waiting for their colonisers (Japan) to keep on handing them food parcels and aid.

South Korean academics could have written articles on how Japan underdeveloped their country and is the reason why South Korea is trapped in poverty or development challenges. R. Guest (2004) said South Korea, which was as poor as Ghana in 1953, is now 20 times richer than Ghana. South Korea is the home of Samsung, LG, Kia, Daewoo, Hyundai Motors, and many other electronic and electrical gadgets. South Korean technology is on equal footing with Japanese technology and at the same level of development as their former colonisers. Today, ex-colonies such as Taiwan, Hong Kong, Malaysia, and Singapore are prosperous and peaceful.

Mbeki M. (2011) said that when the elite has its power threatened by foreigners who are more powerful than itself, one of the ways it attempts to survive is by obtaining the capability that the foreigners have and, in the process, developing its country's economy. According to Molefi Mbeki, this was how Japan developed modern industries, and the interstate wars in Europe forced many of Europe's rulers to develop sectors that gave their countries the industrial capacity to withstand these wars and protect their regimes. This is also how South Korea grew their economy. The African economy has been threatened by Europe, the USA, and Asia; what are African leaders doing about it? Contact helps in bringing in foreign investment. It helps bring in foreign experts to grow the economy if there is good governance. Molefi Mbeki said that acquiring expertise from foreign countries helps. Many experts came to Africa to assist in increasing the economy only to be corrupted by the system, or sometimes corrupt the system.

Colonial rulership should not be exonerated from the development challenges in Africa, but the vision and determination needed for Africa's development are in the hands of African leaders. The development challenges in Africa require determined leaders that are accountable and transparent. I remember vividly when I turned 27 years old. Our ancestors marked this age group for the "wearing cloth" ceremony (initiation to manhood) in my community. In some other Igbo communities, the age is as low as 23 years and might be higher up to 30 to 32 years. This ceremony signifies readiness to attend the Oha Na Eze (Community General Assembly Meetings) meeting in Igbo land, where decisions are taken and negotiations occur. My father told me, "This is an age when you make your own decisions, to start a family and look after your family's affairs when you get married. We are like brothers from now on, even though I am your father. I can consult you if I need help. If you need my help, don't shy away from consulting me". I realised that from that moment onwards, I was on my own. His statement indicated to me the state of a totally independent person without interference unless based on consultation and negotiation.

The independence of the 1960s should have brought to the minds of the leaders and political elites the urgent need for socioeconomic liberation, responsibilities, and positive consequences of a free and sovereign state. Instead, the independence of African countries has led to dictatorships in many countries, where leaders ignored rules and regulations set down in their constitutions for their personal gains. Political systems were hijacked, and opposing views were stifled, giving rise to abuse of power and tyranny by pseudo-leaders in many countries.

3.2 Pseudo-leader

The West colonised Africa by force, and the British colonists introduced indirect rule in their African colonies while the French established direct control. The direct administration by French colonial masters collapsed most of the good numbers of the already existing institutions in pre-colonial Africa. Similarly, the few political institutions that the British allowed to remain in its colonies were mere puppets for the benefit of the colonial governments. Whether by direct French rule or British indirect rule, the impact of colonial leadership in Africa was devastating to the economy and social well-being and impacted the lives of Africans. The question is, "Should we still blame colonial rule for Africa's economic challenges after many years of independence?" No, but the actions of bogymen influence Africans. Nevertheless, the destiny of Africans is in their hand. A 50-year-old man is no longer a child; many African countries have attended independence for over 50 years.

Blaming colonialism is like saying Africans do not have brains and that we cannot make our own decisions. This is a fallacy. The problem the continent has is that many pseudo-leaders are championing the development of the continent. Pseudo-leaders are leaders of fake identity, deceitfulness, and pretence. They are leaders who allow their consciousness to be derailed by greediness, religion, tribalism, ego, and power. Many African leaders would accept non-strategic ideas from Western institutions or individuals that negatively impact African society because of corrupt mindsets, religions, and tribes. Naomi Klein explained how the Structural Adjustment Programme was used to collapse many developing countries' economies.

One of the IMF senior economists, Davison Budhoo, who designed the Structural Adjustment Programme in Latin America and Africa throughout the 1980s, said that everything we did from 1983 headlong was based on our new sense of assignment to have the South "privatised" or die towards the end, we ignominiously created economic bedlam in Latin America and Africa (Klein 2007). Could it be concluded that accepting SAP indicated a lack of confidence in African economists? Does it show the inability of African economists or the need for African leaders to entrust African economists with a chance to develop African-oriented economic policies and theories that speak on our unique economic conditions and challenges? If Africa could rely on our unique economic ideas and policies based on Africa's economic conditions, Africa could not have been vulnerable to SAP's economic conditions. The SAP conditions opened the domestic economy to vulnerability. It allowed foreign interference without much scrutiny from the government. Howard Stein states that African economies have performed poorly throughout adjustment. The question from Howard Stein's statement is why it performed poorly. Is it because of the policy or bad leadership? Alternatively, is it a combination of adjustment policy and bad leadership? I argue that it is bad leadership, not the policy. A good leader should be able to identify bad policies and develop their own policy with his team for his vision and his government's economic agenda.

Embracing all forms of economic theories from Western countries is a sign of weak leadership. This situation does not help develop local potential and resources for economic benefits and growth. For decades, African countries have failed to create economic theories based on sound research findings that speak on each country's social and economic condition.

Pseudo-leaders are leaders of disaster. They are leaders who make policies to profit them without thinking of the impact of the policies years beyond them. They develop guidelines for the interest of a few business elites, which influence the economy of their countries. Pseudo-leaders use public resources for their own family benefits and the benefits of their cronies. Pseudo-leaders are African development nightmares. It is what the Igbo proverb refers to that a witch cried in the night, and a child died in the morning.

Pseudo-leaders are dictatorial and flourish under unfair elections. The table below shows countries that had or still have long-serving pseudo-presidents. All the countries involved are experiencing severe economic hardships.

Let's examine another type of pseudo and undemocratic leaders. There were countries in Africa that experienced military rule since independence, listed in Table 4.4. The countries have severe economic challenges despite some economic growth.

The countries mentioned in Tables 3.3 and 3.4 have experienced, and many are still experiencing, severe economic challenges because of weak leadership and undemocratic tendencies. Some leaders wallow in ignorance and do not understand transparency and accountability. The worst among them were those that transformed from military leaders and rebel leaders to civilian presidents through fraudulent elections, such as in Uganda under Yoweri Museveni, Burkina Faso under Blaise Compaore, and Congo DR under Kabila. They are a burden to social and economic development and integration. Their transformation from violent

Table 3.3 Longest serving president in Africa, past and present in 2023

Country	*President*	*Number of years*
Gabon	Omar Bongo	1967 and died in August 2009 (42 years in power), and his son took over the government
Cameroon	Paul Biya	1982 till 2022 (40 years), the former leader ruled for almost 27 years. Cameroon has been led by two presidents since its independence
Zimbabwe	Robert Mugabe	1980 till 2017 (37 years), headed by one president since independence
Swaziland	King Mswati (took power at the age of 18)	Monarchy (as long as the king lives)
Libya	Momar Gaddafi	1969 till 2011, when he was removed from power by a popular uprising (43 years in power)
Egypt	Muhammad Mubarak	1981 till he was ousted by a popular uprising in 2011 (30 years)
Angola	Jose dos Santos	1979 till 2017 (38 years)
Burkina Faso	Blaise Compaore	1987 till 2014 (27 years)
Chad	Idris Deby	1991 till 2020 (29 years)
Congo	Sassou Nguesso	1979 to 1992, then 1997 to 2020 (35 years)
Equatorial Guinea	Teodoro Obiang Mbasogo	1979 till 2022 (43 years)
Eritrea	Isaias Afewerki	1993 till 2022 (29 years)
Ethiopia	Meles Zenawi	1991 till 2012 (21 years)
Gambia	Yahya Jammeh	1994 till 2017 (23 years)
Guinea Bissau	Vieira Joao	1980 to 2003, 2005 till 2014 (32 years)
Mali	Toure Amadou	1991 to 2012 (21 years)
Morocco	King Mohammed VI	Monarchy state (as long as the king lives)
Nigeria	Sani Abacha, Ibrahim Babangida, Mahmoud Buhari	1983 to 1998 and 2015 to 2023
Somali		Almost the start of anarchy
Sudan	Omar Hassan al-Bashir	1989 till 2017 (28 years)
Tunisia	Zine Ben Ali	1987 till he was removed in the uprising of 2011 (24 years)
Uganda	Yoweri Museveni	1986 till 2020 (34 years)

Source: Author 2022

leadership to civilian presidents creates gaps between the governed and the government. A Chinese proverb says, "The Mountains are high, and the emperor is far away". They are agents of suppression of freedom of speech

Table 3.4 Countries that experienced military rule in Africa and the period

Countries	*Periods*
Nigeria	1966–1979 and 1983 to 1999
Burundi	1966 to 1993
Congo	1968 to 1992
DRC	1965 to 2006
Algeria	1965 to 1994
Gambia	1994 to 1997
Liberia	1980 to 1990
Chad	1975 to 1991
Equatorial Guinea	1968 till present
Ghana	1966–1969, 1972–1979, 1981–1993
Libya	1969 till 2011
Uganda	1971 to 1986 (present president a former rebel leader)
Burkina Faso	1966 to 1991, the current president, a former military leader, transformed into a democratic leader and was removed by a popular uprising in 2014
Egypt	1952 till 2011
Central Africa Republic	1966 till 1993
Ethiopia	1974 till 1991
Guinea	1984 to 1991
Madagascar	1972 to 1975
Niger	1974–1989, 1996–1999
Somalia	1969–1991, then local militants
Sudan	1958–1964, 1969–1985, 1989 till present
Mauritania	1978–1992, 2005–2007
Sierra Leone	1992–1996, 1997–1998

Source: Author 2022

and press. These countries are known for using force, hijacking government institutions, and human rights abuses.

African pseudo-leaders take government as a family possession because of corrupt activities. These leaders appoint their family members and cronies to various positions to protect their self-interest, which is rampant in Nigeria. They do not know that nepotism is corruption. In some countries, fathers' death has led to some of their siblings taking over the government through undemocratic means and was rampant in French colonies, for example, in DR Congo, Gabon, and Togo. Politics is a scheme to get rich in Africa, where politicians are more prosperous than entrepreneurs. How can a country develop in such a situation? Pseudo-leadership has failed to reform African economies, due to mismanagement and corruption. They have refused to bow out for new ideas. Their refusals to yield power are driven by fear of prosecution and ethnic suppression, which they have engineered for a long time. Pseudo-leaders prey on ethnic, religious, and political loyalty against the development of their countries. The pseudo-leaders indulge in the politics of hate, deceit, and revenge. Instead of developing ideas for serving their countries, they are busy pursuing selfish control of the state. To achieve their political gains, they promote politics of favouritism.

Opposition parties are not spared from their own form of dictatorial tendencies. The leaders of many opposition parties have been in office for more than ten years, some for more than two decades, without allowing free and fair internal party elections. This form of despotism also indicates that opposition parties are like the ruling political parties. Many parties spring up on a tribal basis rather than national coverage with plural tribal integration.

Many pseudo-politicians promote selfish interests through extreme religious and ethnic mobilisation for votes rather than ideas. This is why, in many political campaigns, they insult each other, castigate character, and buy votes instead of political parties selling their ideas through manifestos. Most times, campaigns for elections are not about the debate on ideas but rather about using the media to spread lies and propaganda, particularly political parties in power. APC government in Nigeria is very good at it.

Africa's political environment always experiences crisis caused by attempts at constitutional amendments to change presidential tenure. Many pseudo-leaders had changed their countries' constitutions to elongate their stay in power as if they were mortals who would rule forever. The purpose of such constitutional amendments and change is to elongate the tenure of a serving president, the goal of which is to promote selfish interests and disoriented governments. The following presidents sought constitutional changes to elongate their presidential stay in power.

1. Djibouti: In April 2010, the Parliament of Djibouti approved a constitutional amendment that allowed President Ismael Omar Guelleh to run for a third term.

2. Cameroon: In April 2008, the parliament amended the constitution, eliminating the number of presidential terms limit. Paul Biya, who had been in power since 1982, was re-elected to a seventh term in October 2018.
3. Uganda: In July 2005, a constitutional reform removed limitations on the number of presidential terms. Yoweri Museveni, who has been in power since 1986, was re-elected in 2011.
4. Chad: In June 2005, a constitutional amendment adopted a controversial referendum that removed the limit to two five-year presidential terms. Idriss Deby Itno, who has been in power since 1990, was re-elected in 2011.
5. Togo: In December 2002, a constitutional amendment smoothened the way for Gnassingbe Eyadema, who has been in power since 1967, to seek another term in 2003. However, in February 2005, he died, and the parliament passed a constitutional revision that allowed his son, Faure Gnassingbe, favoured by the army, to be sworn in as president. International pressure pushed him to resign, but he was declared the winner of the subsequent election.
6. In Angola, in January 2010, a constitutional amendment allowed indirect suffrage by parliamentarians. This allowed Angola president Jose Eduardo dos Santos, who has been in power since 1979, to be sworn in in 2012 after his party's victory in legislative elections.
7. Many other presidents who tried constitutional amendment for elongation of the presidential term but failed were Zambia's former president Frederick Chiluba, who was forced to backstep after popular pressure, and Malawi's Bakili Muluzi, who was blocked by the parliament in 2002 from seeking a third mandate. Burkina Faso's former president, Blaise Compaore, resigned after a failed constitutional change attempt to allow him to stay in power after being in control for over 30 years.

Africa has witnessed up to four decades of sit-tight pattern in government and manipulation of the constitution for tenure extension by many African leaders that led to protracted conflict and truncation of civil rule. In desperate attempts to clinch power, many leaders are transforming ethnic groups and cultural groups into fragmented political parties. Presently, ethnic nationalities are progressing at an alarming rate to political parties and pressure groups that breed undemocratic principles and threaten other ethnic groups. Similarly, the transformation of ethnic groups into political parties and pressure groups has promoted and encouraged mediocrity by appointing unqualified people to leadership. Often, ethnic groups have pitched against one another for selfish political interests instead of being unified for development. Countries with rampant ethnic politics are Nigeria, Kenya, Cameroon, Zimbabwe, DRC, Tanzania, Liberia, and Uganda.

Ethnicity may not be all bad within the democratic structures of a country, as ethnicity can play a vital role in developing a plural state with good citizenship. Ethnicity can create solid nationhood if positively enabled. Ethnic nationhood creates development encompassing different forms of economic potential that would lead to growth and enhance states' image.

In the 1980s and 1990s, changes in political structures affected Africa severely. Foreign investments suffered in countries like Nigeria and Ghana, where leaders changed quickly because of military interventions from the 1960s to the 1990s. The leadership changes often lead to policies changing to suit some of the leaders' hidden interests rather than national ones.

Pseudo-leaders are leaders of short-sightedness, and they care less about small businesses' social and economic welfare. In Nigeria and South Africa, small traders were constantly harassed and evicted from their vending stands without making any proper arrangement for relocation. Small businesses were crushed with price controls that allowed the government to effectively confiscate most of their merchandise. For example, in 1984 in Nigeria, Muhammadu Buhari, a military junta, forced small businesses to sell at a specific price below profit making, which caused severe hardship. Many street traders had been detained, their goods seized, and trading spots destroyed.

Small businesses and vendors in many African cities face stiff government regulations. In South Africa and Nigeria, informal traders marketing local farm produce often met strict government policies and regulations. In Lagos in 2013, the state government headed by Mr. Fashola deported informal traders from Lagos in Nigeria to Anambra State in the name of ridding the city of the destitute. You begin to wonder how you deport someone in his own country. In October 2013, the City of Johannesburg removed many informal traders from the Johannesburg CBD without alternative relocation plans. The traders were pointing fingers at the mayor of Johannesburg Metropolitan Council, whose mother was once a casual trader in the city. Although the situation was restored in certain areas, many lost their goods through confiscation by the municipality.

The eviction of informal traders in Lagos, Harare, Nairobi, Johannesburg, and many African towns is disheartening. Seizing informal traders' goods and products without warning devastates their families' livelihoods. These are cities battling with increasing unemployment. If there had been an alternative relocation plan from the government, the consequences of their action could have been minimised. There is nothing wrong with creating business regulation, but it must also be favourable to small businesses. The continent's citizens are facing seizures at the hands of those who should be directing and leading them.

Africa's development challenges, in part, are a result of the scramble for wealth by many predator elites who emerged due to poor governance that has dominated African governments since independence. These predictor elites see the state as a source of wealth accumulation. They do not know the state as a means of serving the citizens through accountable and transparent government but rather as a high premium leeway to easy accessibility to the source of wealth accumulation. Their perception of the state as a source of wealth accumulation leads them to seek power, including fostering ethnic sectarianism and political repression. They are politicians who seek to win the next election rather than develop Africa for the next generation to be better.

In Africa, many ruling political parties have often deliberately derailed governance by centralising powers at the national government level. It is to take control of power and functions by distributing resources. Centralisation of power enhances authoritarian government, where the function of other tiers of government, such as state/provincial and local government duties, is controlled by the national government or the presidents and their cronies. The executive's centralisation of power helps them dictate what happens to the rest of the country. The pseudo-leaders do this through unequal distributions of resources. It eliminates a true federal or regional system of government where regions or states can develop their potential for economic growth of the country, which is a more sustainable way of governance and development.

African pseudo-leaders are devoid of ideas that should revolutionise use of natural resources for the benefit of economic growth and promote sustainable income. They prey on communities' resources, leading to poverty and damaging sustainable livelihoods. Instead of exploitation of natural resources to encourage sustainable development, it escalates mismanagement, corruption, and lack of accountability. These have been possible due to decades of military coups, dictatorships, and changes in the constitution to elongate power. Many African countries where there is the mining of gold, diamonds, and oil have witnessed dictatorship, conflicts, executive rascality, and impunity because of natural resources gains. Paul Biya has led Cameroon for more than four decades; De Santos, the former president of Angola; Teodoro Obiang Mbasogo of Equatorial Guinea, Nigeria, under the military leadership of Congo in the past four decades and former president of Gabon—Omar Bongo. Up to six African countries have endured bloody conflicts fuelled by the scramble for diamonds and gold for the past three decades. Examples are Angola, DRC, Liberia, Sierra Leone, Central Africa Republic, and the Republic of Congo. The killing of more than 34 miners in Marikana, Northwest Province of South Africa, in 2012 was an outcome of mining activities.

Despite the abuses of miners that go unabated, the mining companies do not spare the environment that sustains the mining communities. There seems to be a systematic disregard by the leaders to protect the environment and natural resources upon which the ethnic groups or citizens sustain their livelihood. This is evident in the destruction and pollution of land and water where oil mining occurs in Nigeria, Cameroon, Angola, Gabon, and other parts of Africa. There are land degradation and soil pollution where solid minerals are mined in Southern Africa. As mining destroys land and pollutes water, what is the future of these communities?

In a statement accredited to Lesiba Seshoka in Sunday Times on 8 April 2012, "A black miner dies, and it is no story; a rhino dies it is a big story". Lesiba Seshoka narrates the agonising condition that black miners face in the mining industry in South Africa. He was not saying that animals should not be taken care of; he was worried about how miners' life has become less valuable to mine owners. It was not up to six months when Lesiba Seshoka's statement was made that more than 34 black miners were killed and 40 wounded in Lonmin in South Africa in what has been termed "Dark August". Lesiba Seshoka's statement is a disturbing statement directed at African leadership and mine operators. It shows the slapdash attitude of some of Africa's leadership towards its people and development. The deplorable conditions these miners lived in led to their demand. The increasing cost of living due to inflation contributed to the suffering of the miners. In the desperate situation to diffuse the miscarriage, the political elites pointed fingers and played a blame game. The only blame goes to the leaders who could not protect their citizens from social and economic abuse through policies and strategies. The situation could have been averted earlier if the stakeholders had acted in good faith and in time through proper negotiation.

Protecting miners and communities from all sorts of mining teething troubles is not a concern to the leaders of Africa. Mining activities in the continent destroy the livelihood support of communities and affect their health; in vain, political leaders turn a blind eye to these unacceptable conditions. There is little or no compensation for communities or individuals affected by mining companies' activities. Some of them, who were compensated, got it through court orders. The BP payout as compensation for the Gulf of Mexico oil spillage in the USA was about $5 billion in entitlements. Then, visit South-South Nigeria's states and see some communities suffering from oil spillage and pollution for decades without receiving little or no compensation. What happened in the Gulf of Mexico is minor compared to what is happening in Nigeria's oil mining areas and other parts of Africa, where mining has been destroying the environment and damaging the sustainable livelihoods of communities for decades while leaders and political elites ignore the situation.

3.3 Judiciary and Human Rights Abuses

The judiciary is vital to the development of a country. Judges play many roles in society; they interpret the law, control the hearing in a courtroom, assess evidence, and ensure that the executive arm of government does not breach the constitution. In some countries, the judiciary is part of the mechanism that monitors executive performance. One of the judiciary's most important duties is ensuring no impartiality in dispensing justice. With a proper judicial system, the achievement of social and economic development will be improved. The twenty-first century has shown that economic and social development is not just about businesses but the rule of law. According to Dakolias (2003, p. 1), "rule of law is in effect when there are:

1. Meaningful and enforceable laws: That means transparency, fairness, and predictability in decisions.
2. When there are enforceable contracts: So that there is the promotion of business and commerce.
3. When there is basic security, That means personal safety and protection of property and an independent judiciary that safeguards both.

4. And finally, when there is access to justice, That means concrete ways to invoke that safeguard".

Dakolias M (2003) further states that if we have these elements, the state can regulate the economy and empower private individuals to contribute to economic development by confidently engaging in business, investments, and other transactions. It, in turn, fosters domestic and foreign investment, creating jobs and reducing poverty. For sustainable development, there must be the rule of law. With the rule of law, social and economic growth will succeed.

Nevertheless, Africans have witnessed how judges become foot-dragging in delivering free and fair judgments because of the interference of leaders and political elites. Executive rascality and impunity frustrate judgment through intimidation and harassment of judges by state security agencies. For example, in Zambia, former president Michael Sata suspended three judges—Supreme Court Justice Philip Musonda, High Court Judge Nigel Mutuna, and Charles Kalimanga—for suspected misconduct in a matter involving his political allies, Director of Public Prosecution (DPP) Mutembo Nchito and Patriotic Front political member Fred M'membe. M'membe, the owner of the Post Newspaper, and Nchito, a director at Zambian Airways, borrowed 14 billion Kwacha from the Development Bank of Zambia, which payment they defaulted, forcing the court to pass judgment against them. In Nigeria, under Buhari led government, Marry Odili, a Supreme Court judge, was harassed by Nigeria state security. In Nigeria, the Supreme Court judge admitted an error but stated they could not review the case they had already judged. An example was Emeka Ihedioha versus Hope Uzodinma, where Hope Uzodinma became a governor through a Supreme Court judgment error. Could five sitting Supreme Court judges possibly make an error, or is it a deliberate action planned by the executives?

Judges have become torn into the flesh of businesses and citizens in some countries because of their corrupt tendencies. Many judges are so corrupt that judgment is passed based on the highest bidder. It is common that a roadside thief will get 10 to 20 years' imprisonment while corrupt politicians who stole billions are given light sentences, which are often suspended, sometimes with fines of less than 5% of what they stole. You ask yourself, between the roadside thief and the corrupt politician, who did more damage to the country. A corrupt politician stole money made for development that could have created jobs and enhanced health and education; in a way, a corrupt politician created the fate of the roadside thief by stealing money that could have created jobs for him or her. Is the justice system terrible, or does the constitution need to be better developed?

In the pursuit of justice and good judgment, human right becomes essential. America's Declaration of Independence on 4 July 1776, highlighted that it is self-evident that all men are created equal and that humans are endowed by their creator with certain inalienable rights, among which are the rights to life, liberty, and pursuit of happiness; these rights are enshrined in almost all the countries in Africa. Therefore, human rights are not a negotiable commodity for the development of a nation, and it is necessary for individuals' socioeconomic emancipation.

Human rights devastation is noticeable in the suppression of the right to life and social and economic choices across Africa, particularly those living in slums and informal settlements in Lagos in Nigeria, Kibera slum in Kenya, former Cowdry Park informal settlement in Zimbabwe, informal settlements in South Africa; those languishing unfairly in prisons in Angola and Nigeria, the women and girls denied access to sexual and reproductive health rights in Burkina Faso, and millions of people who are still fleeing from armed conflicts and poverty in Africa.

Social and economic abuses are underestimated and overlooked in the continent. This abuse has led to many deaths because of poor health facilities and lack of access to infrastructure that will enhance a decent life. Without better and accessible infrastructure, human rights are trampled upon, and better living will not be attainable. The abuse of women's rights comes in different forms—denial of access to better reproductive health facilities, which leads to the death of pregnant women. Forcing young girls into unwanted or early marriages. Forcing women into prostitution, most times, leads to drug abuse. Many African women suffer sexual violence, such as rape, and restricted access to various opportunities. Many of these abuses are due to society's stereotypes because of weak leadership.

The right to decent housing has been ignored in almost all African countries except, perhaps, South Africa. The South African government is trying to ensure that citizens can access subsidised decent housing or service stands. The drive towards access to decent housing in South Africa is good, but the system in which it is provided still faces some challenges. In other parts of Africa, it is not their leaders' vision to ensure their citizens have access to decent housing or shelter. Instead, in many African cities, slums and ghettos are developing at alarming rates while governments are busy bulldozing them down and rendering the occupants homeless without providing alternative accommodations. In 2009, Amnesty International highlighted the plight of tens of thousands left homeless in N'Djamena, Chad, after forced evictions. The inhabitants of slums in Cairo, Egypt, remained at risk of being killed by landslides or other hazards due to the failure to provide adequate housing. At Kibera in Kenya, one of the largest slums in Africa, you will not fail to ask yourself the essence of living in the world. Maroko, a poor neighbourhood in Lagos, was demolished to make way for high-income residential developments, and more than 200,000 people lost a place they call home and a source of income. Thousands of informal dwellers died in Sierra Leone in August 2017 from a mud flood. In Africa, informal settlements and slum dwellers have lost billions of dollars in properties through fire and floods. It is a typical failure of planning by leadership. No abuse is more significant than denying citizens access to basic housing or service stands. Demolishing slums without providing alternative accommodation in Africa is very common, affecting these people's social and economic linkages. Millions of Africans living in slums and low-income neighbourhoods have not experienced what it means to have access to essential services such as clean water, sanitation, health care, education, and effective policing. In many countries, the authorities ignore their predicament and exclude them from service delivery and infrastructure development. Discrimination in providing access to infrastructure and housing is against the right to decent living. It is disempowering people socially and economically. Discrimination is the primary driver of poverty, reflected in the allocation of government budgets and spending.

The recklessness of security officers and the rascality of the government in power led to the death of many demonstrators in Africa. An example is the EndSars protest in Nigeria against police brutality that led to the killing of more than 200 protesters. The impunity of governments in power leads to the silencing, arresting, and killing of journalists in Africa. Many refugees and migrants of African origin have suffered at the hands of police and immigration officers in Africa, and some are detained without any reason. In places like Tanzania, Uganda, and Kenya, asylum seekers often were forcibly returned home, facing more problems because of ongoing economic hardship, conflicts, or both. In South Africa, law enforcement agents' responses to xenophobic attacks were inadequate and led to the loss of lives and properties. Angola has expelled more than 100,000 DRC citizens from their country to face more significant dangers in the DRC, and Zimbabwe recently expelled Malawians without apparent reasons.

One of the behemoths that beleaguered the continent is failing to exercise the fundamental right of one's opinion, the ability to say one's mind without prejudice. When Africans fail to discuss what needs to be addressed, keeping quiet in the face of atrocities is romancing with the nemesis of weak leadership. In the face of bogymen's irresponsible governance, silence and docility is a failure to hold bogymen accountable. Ratcliffe (2016) cited Harriet Stowe's quote, "the harshest tears shed over graves are for words left unsaid and actions left undone". The impact of the docile citizenry has led to leaders living in ignorance of their challenges and false hope in the realities. The importance of truth must be considered. "Authentic and honest internal communication results in better, faster decisions and actions. It also builds a culture of trust and collaboration where opposing views are debated and more effective solutions and innovations are created" (Harris 2006, p. 1). Truth enhances development and builds trust that leads to effective and innovative development. "Plato is dear to me, but dearer still is truth" (Ratcliffe 2016) quoted Aristotle 384–399 BC, the reason Igbos will say ezi okwu bu ndu (Truth is life). Honesty and truth are the only ways to sustain good governance while embracing development. Therefore, the right to expression of thought or freedom of speech becomes paramount to a society's development. Who wants to invest in an area where human rights are not observed or police and security personnel kill, detain, and intimidate without proper legal procedures? No person would want to invest where his property and life are in danger. Addressing human rights abuse in Africa will be needed to gain business confidence.

CHAPTER 4

Technology and Deindustrialisation

4.1 Technology Underdevelopment

With technology, modern life would be more manageable. Technology has provided the means by which we can speed up production. Technology makes the world smaller by bridging distances. Technology has changed how we communicate and the built environment, improving the education and health systems. Thus, with the advent of technological advancement that has engulfed the world, African leaders are yet to fully embrace it through research and innovations for sustainable development. The continent's contribution to global technological advancement is minimal compared to other continents such as Europe, the North America, and Asia. The massive importation of technology services and hardware and poor investment in technology advancement through research and innovations result from the misplacement of priorities and corruption that diminishes resources.

The limitations in innovation and research result from weak leadership; Africans have proven themselves to be innovative, creative, and adept in research development outside Africa. Growing up in a rural area (Ihitteafoukwu Mbaise) in Imo State, Nigeria, I am among many Africans who believed that white men invented everything on earth. When I was in secondary school, it was a huge surprise when the news broke that Damian Anyanwu from Mbaise in the Imo State of Nigeria—developed a radio

C. E. Osuigwe, *Leadership and Economic Development Challenges in Post-Colonial Africa*, Sustainable Development Goals Series,
https://doi.org/10.1007/978-3-031-45663-3_4

short-wave transmitter powered by herbs. As I grew up, I enquired about the fate of Damian Anyanwu in Nigeria, and I found out that he migrated to the USA, where he founded a research institute called Damian Anyanwu Research Center Inc (DARCI). This happened because the Nigerian leaders needed to encourage and support the research and the idea. The stories of modern inventions by Africans in the Western world, like Philip Emeagwali, are known.

The success story of Engineer Ezekiel Izuogu in developing the first indigenous African car, Z-600, is known in Nigeria. The car was launched in 1997, and 90% of the car's components were made locally with a proposed price of $2000, which could have been the world's cheapest car at the time. Mass production of the vehicle was planned under Izuogu Motors, and because of political hurdles and financial constraints, the car did not proceed past its prototype stage.

Africans are more than capable of contributing to technological inventions and innovations. Contribution to technological inventions and innovations would have been possible if leaders and political elites could plan and provide a sound social, economic, and political environment. For instance, during the presidency of Umaru Yaradua, Nigeria experienced its first African-made motor vehicles built by Innoson Motors.

Recently, individual efforts have led to some outstanding inventions and innovations in Africa by black people, such as:

1. Charging shoe that was invented by a Kenyan called Anthony Mutua. The technology is used to charge cell phone batteries using pedestrian power.
2. Cardiopad was invented by a Cameroonian entrepreneur called Marc Arthur. It is a medical computer tablet used to examine the heart.
3. The Please Call Me Concept was invented by Nkosana Makate.
4. Mobile Money Transfer, The Malaria pf/PAN (pLDH) Test Kit, SavvyLoo, Mubser, Mellowcabs, Cardiopad, Saphonian Zero-Blade Wind Convertor, The iCow app, and Bus Transport powered by Solar System, among others.

In pre-colonial times and modern times, Africans have contributed to technological development. During the pre-colonial era, there were inventions such as glass tools used for shaving, found along Africa's Njoro River in Kenya; a water pipe known as the "Bong" created around 1460 BC in Ethiopia; iron ore smelted in furnaces in 450 BC by the Nok People of Nigeria. The first university in the world: the University of Sankore was in Africa, and the first-ever library was founded in Timbuktu in Mali with stacks of books, some dating more than 500 years.

There have been inventions or contributions to innovations by black people in other countries outside Africa, particularly in the USA. This proves that black people can do their best under any good leadership. The list below shows some black inventions or black-assisted inventions and innovations:

1. Garret A. Morgan invented belt fasteners for sewing machines, gas masks, and automatic traffic signalling systems.
2. Elija McCoy invented a drip cup for oiling factory machinery, a lubricator cup, and a lawn sprinkler.
3. Dr Raphael E. Armattoe, the Ghanaian scientist, found the cure for the water-borne guinea worm disease.
4. Robert E. Shurney designed the wire mesh tyres for the buggy used in the Apollo 15 moon landing.
5. Jan Ernst Matzeliger invented the lasting machine for the shoemaking industry.
6. Granville T. Woods invented a telephone transmitter that transformed the quality and distance that sound could travel. He also invented the railway telegraph system and improved it to an overhead electric system to power trains.
7. Richard Spikes established the automatic gearshift for cars.
8. George Carruthers, an astrophysicist of NASA, developed the Far Ultraviolet Camera used on the Apollo 16 mission that gave the world a groundbreaking view of the moon in the 1970s.
9. Fredrick M. Jones invented the automatic refrigeration system for long-distance trucks.
10. James West, with Gerhard M. Sessler, invented the foil-electric microphone.
11. Dr Patricia E. Bath, an ophthalmologist, invented the Laserphoto Probe.
12. Dr. Philip Emeagwali 1989, a Nigerian emigré to the USA, performed the world's fastest computer computation.

13. Mark Dean, an electrical engineer with his colleague at IBM, developed ISA Systems Bus, an interface that connects multiple devices, like modems and printers, to computers.
14. The chemist Percy L. Julian led the way in treating Alzheimer's disease and glaucoma when his experiments broke new ground in 1933. This was possible when his research into the synthesis of physostigmine, a drug to treat glaucoma, improved memory in Alzheimer's patients and served as an antidote to nerve gas.
15. Dotseyi Sogah, a Ghanaian émigré, in 1980 with his colleagues Owen Webster and William B. Farnham, developed a new technique for synthesising polymers and petroleum compounds to make plastic paints and synthetic fibres.
16. Benjamin Banneker was an astronomer who made the first clock in America.
17. Lewis Latimer improved upon Thomas Edison's light bulb, which, until Latimer came in, had a lifespan of only 20 minutes. Latimer fashioned the carbon filament that vastly improved the lifespan of the incandescent light bulb, and in 1882, invented a machine to manufacture the carbon filaments.
18. Madam C. J. Walker, America's first woman millionaire, invented the Hot Comb, the Wonderful Hair Grower, the Vegetable Shampoo, and Glossine.
19. Ron Headley invented an ecocharger. It is a cleaner diesel engine emission system that improves the performance of diesel cars because it reduces smoke emission fuel consumption.
20. Tope Awotona is the founder and CEO of Calendly, a functional and effective scheduling tool that helps people schedule meetings, appointments, and events without all the back-and-forth emails. The app is currently valued at over $3 billion. Tope grew up in Lagos, Nigeria and moved to the USA, where he graduated from the University of Georgia.
21. Chinedu Echeruo founded a startup, HopStop, a pioneering travel app that helped millions of users navigate public transportation in major metropolitan areas worldwide; Apple Inc. acquired the city transit app in 2013 for $1 billion.

The above information shows that Africans contributed to inventions and innovations in the West than in Africa. The challenge in Africa is the political, social, and economic situations that do not allow sound minds to achieve their dreams. If the right leaders and political elites determine and define the social, economic, and political environment, Africans can do more than other people do in other parts of the world. Poor innovations and inventions are reducing industrialisation while enhancing the deindustrialisation of the continent.

4.2 Deindustrialisation

Industrialisation is a crucial component of socioeconomic development, and it plays a significant role in employment and leads to vibrant economic activities. In pre-colonial Africa, industrialisation of the continent was taking place. Chirikure (2018), in his publication "Pre-colonial Metallurgy and Mining across Africa", highlighted that Africans were involved in mining in the pre-colonial times. There was industrial mining of iron, gold, bronze, and silver, smelting industries, cotton fabric dying of clothes and brass refining. There was agricultural industrialisation through storage systems and irrigation. Due to the industrial development in pre-colonial Africa, there was international trade between African kingdoms and empires to exchange goods and services.

On the eve of the independence of most African countries, the zeal and energy of post-independence led to a new era of industrial development in most cities and towns. The drive by the liberators of colonial territories in the industrialisation of African cities and towns was enormous. Industries, companies, and institutions were scrambling for graduates from higher education institutions for employment and empowerment.

What happened to Africa's industrialisation momentum or drive after one decade of these efforts from the eve of independence? The argument is not saying there have not been investments and building of new industries in Africa, but the rate of industrialisation is meagre while many industries have closed. The main culprit in deindustrialisation is Africa's heavy reliance on importing finished goods and services and the need for infrastructure development. In the 1980s, Nigeria had two car assembly plants—Peugeot and Volkswagen—to give an insight into deindustrialisation in Africa. It was expected that the number of car assembly plants or manufacturing should increase by now. In the 1990s, Volkswagen's assembly plant was closed, and Peugeot assembly plant's capacity was drastically reduced. The deindustrialisation of Nigeria continued from 1983 to 1999.

The NNPC that was refining oil products stopped during this period. Instead, Nigeria started the importation of refined petroleum and oil products. Nigeria Airways used to be the best in Africa, competing with Ethiopian Airways. Nigeria Airways has been grounded for the past two to three decades and does not have a single aircraft to its name. The Ajaokuta and Delta steel companies in Nigeria, built by the government to drive the industrial revolution, stopped not until 2014 when Ajaokuta started producing at a low capacity. The companies suffered at the hands of policymakers, and one wonders whether Nigeria ever had leaders that had the country's long-term interests at heart. However, between 2011 and 2015, the automobile policies of the government of Goodluck Ebele Jonathan attracted auto manufacturers such as Nissan and Hyundai to set up assembly lines and encouraged the already existing first African-made brand, the Innoson motors.

The former Zimbabwean prime minister Morgan Tsvangirai said that President Mugabe's preparation for Zimbabwe's 32nd birthday celebration for independence is "repugnant", and he said, "Fighters who died to end colonial rule in 1980 will only be proud of us if we bring back the noise in our silent factories". Unfortunately, Zimbabwe, previously one of Africa's most significant industrial countries, has declined significantly. Mbeki (2009) highlighted in his book *Advocate of Poverty* that Africa is plagued with abandoned industries. He cited an example of Kafue in Zambia, which used to be a hive of activity but today is a ghost town. In 2004, the United Nations Industrial Development Organization (UNIDO) released a damning report on the deindustrialisation of Africa. According to the report, sub-Saharan Africa has deindustrialised since 1970. The report states that many developing countries in Asia have improved, which shows in the increase of export of manufactured goods, unlike that of sub-Saharan Africa, which did not increase. The report attributed this negative output to the capital flight taking place in the continent. The report states that in all the regions of the world, sub-Saharan Africa has the highest capital flight. Accordingly, in 1990, Africa had a higher proportion of its private wealth outside Africa. It was a shock to learn that by 1999, Nigeria's personal wealth of 107 billion dollars was estimated to be outside Africa. During the 1990s, Uganda experienced one of the highest capital flights until it could curtail it in 2000. Deindustrialisation is the consequence of bad leadership. The results of bad leadership have failed to transform Africa's potential and natural resources into industrial development by creating an enabling environment for private investments.

CHAPTER 5

Education and Labour

5.1 Education and Artisan Development

To highlight the damage done to education or lack of foresight to the educational development of Africa, it would be necessary to examine the literacy rate in Africa and compare it to other continents. Table 5.1 compares the literacy rate and enrolment statistics between sub-Saharan Africa and different sub-regions.

Table 5.1 shows that total adult literacy is 62%, which means 38% of Africans are illiterate. It is overwhelming to know that sub-Saharan Africa is by far worse than other regions in the percentage of adult literacy. Different continents are above 90% of adult literacy. Table 5.1 also indicates that enrolment for primary education in sub-Saharan Africa, which stands at 72%, is poor compared to other regions. These problems are compounded by poor motivation, incomprehensive government policies, poor accountability, transparency, and corruption. Furthermore, let's examine the rates of enrolment in primary schools.

The United Nations Sustainable Development Goals (SDGs) cannot be achieved, with most countries' primary school completion being less than 60% of the population. The result in Table 5.2 shows the poor commitment of Africa's leaders to educational development that will ensure that every child has a primary education. In Burkina Faso, Mali, and Niger, half of the population has not attended primary school, while in Senegal,

C. E. Osuigwe, *Leadership and Economic Development Challenges in Post-Colonial Africa*, Sustainable Development Goals Series,
https://doi.org/10.1007/978-3-031-45663-3_5

Table 5.1 Comparison of literacy and primary school enrolment

Continent	*Total adult literacy rate (%), 2005–2010*	*Primary school net enrolment ratio (%) 2007–2009*
East Asia and the Pacific	94%	95%
Latin America and the Caribbean	91%	95%
Sub-Saharan Africa	62%	76%

Source: UNICEF: Comparison indicators

41.81% of its population has not attended primary school. In Nigeria, the figure is 21.84%. Considering the continent's social, economic, and political challenges, more must be done to encourage access to education. The biggest challenge is that many of the enrolment numbers in primary school still need to be completed, as indicated in Table 5.2. Nigeria is the only country with a record of 80% of children that went to school and completed their primary school education. Countries such as Uganda, Malawi, Rwanda, Kenya, and Senegal had below 50% of children who completed their primary education. Some countries' enrolments in schools are very good, while the completion of primary schooling is very poor, like in the case of Uganda, Rwanda, and Malawi. The data is an embarrassment going by the economic and social challenges the continent is facing. Education is necessary for the development of the continent to be sustainable.

In Africa, the level of illiteracy has led to many people failing to hold their leaders accountable. High illiteracy results from bad policies and strategies or poor implementation of sound policies and procedures. When schools are not built closer to poor and rural communities; when textbooks are not supplied to schools; when depilated school buildings and furniture are not repaired and refurbished; when there are not enough books in the libraries, when pupils and students walk many kilometres to go to school daily; when teachers have no resources or fewer resources to teach; these are deliberate actions by the leaders to keep literacy low, and they are affecting the growth and development of Africa. Knowledge is power. With high literacy levels, it is easier for Africans to call the leadership to order. Additionally, when there is a high level of illiteracy, there is also a high possibility of conflict because of ignorance. A good education will minimise conflict because it empowers youths and encourages them to be involved in meaningful engagements.

Table 5.2 Primary school statistics in Africa

Country	*Never attended*	*Drop out without primary school*	*Over age, still in primary*	*Completed primary*
Kenya 2003	9.11%	16.15%	45.36%	38.49%
Senegal	41.81%	30.31	21.59	48.20
Niger 2006	56.35	29.90	7.11	62.99
Mali 2006	50.86	18.64	14.38	66.98
Madagascar 2003	13.71	30.54	4.40	65.07
Cameroon 2004	8.43	12.89	15.48	71.63
Ghana 2003	11.33	9.44	11.56	79.00
Malawi 2004	5.61	27.76	40.42	31.83
Nigeria 2003	21.84	3.19	13.15	83.66
Rwanda 2005	8.11	47.02	36.99	15.99
Uganda 2006	5.54	22.41	39.54	38.06
Burkina Faso 2003	58.28	27.21	1.93	70.86
Benin 2006	27.57	17.92	9.81	72.27
Zambia 2007	2.22	11.80	26.70	61.50
Tanzania 2007	7.37	11.29	24.26	64.45

Source: Education for All Global Monitoring Report, 2011. Regional Overview: Sub-Saharan Africa

Note: (1) The proportion of children who dropped out without completing primary school is estimated by the total number of 16- and 17-year-olds who had dropped out and not completed primary school relative to the number of 16- and 17-year-olds who attended school. (2) The proportion of over-age children still in primary school is estimated by the ratio of 16- and 17-year-olds who were still in primary school at the time of the survey

Getting an education does not mean everyone must attend school to get educated. Vocational training is a form of education that brings learning closer to people. Vocational training is a form of education that allows the recipient to learn and acquire skills through participating in production activities. It is a means of transferring skills or entrepreneurship from a business owner to an apprentice. The vocational system of improving skills had worked well in pre-colonial Africa and is presently in Asia. However, to some extent, it still works in West Africa without government development policies. Vocational education helped Indians and the Chinese develop small-scale manufacturing and service industries. In China, pre-employment, job transfer, and apprentice and on-the-job training programmes provide vocational education and training. In 1996, China introduced an educational reform called Vocational Education and

Training (VET). The primary purpose of VET is to promote employment, economic growth, and social advancement through skill development, job training, and empowerment.

During the pre-colonial period, vocational training helped shape the time's development. Vocational training in the pre-colonial period was steered through the age-grades, family lineage, trade mentoring, and talent training. The pre-colonial people were taught social etiquette, agricultural methods, and other knowledge and skills that ensured the smooth running of their communities. The male children learned practical skills by observing and imitating their elders, perfecting such skills as they matured into manhood, and passing them on to their own children when they became heads of their own households. The present poor vocational education and training is because of the insensitive behaviour of the leaders towards enhancing sustainable development, particularly in rural communities. Where there is vocational training, implementations need more efficient management.

Selassie's (1963) Acceptance Speech as the First President of the Organization of African Union (OAU) highlighted the importance of VET. He said, "A massive effort must be launched in the educational and cultural field which will not only raise the level of literacy and provide a cadre of skilled and trained technicians requisite to our growth and development, but as well acquaint us one with another". He further itemised that serious consideration should be given to establishing an African university, sponsored by all African states, where future leaders of Africa will be trained in an atmosphere of continental brotherhood. African institutions should be supra-national aspects of African life directed towards the goal of complete African unity. One way to achieve Haile Selassie's dream is to have a vision of developing raw skills based on pre-colonial ideas such as skill transfer, the concept of brotherhood (Ubuntu and Nwanne), and participatory decision-making.

Colonial education equipped our fathers and grandfathers to think that the social characteristics of Europeans were better than those of Africans, which was unfair. It created a situation where the colonists used a few Africans to exploit Africa's resources, perpetuating colonial political and economic strategies and agendas. Do we dwell on this and continue to blame the Europeans? The answer is no because it has been over four decades since many Africans gained independence. By now, Africans should know how to do things in their own ways.

The copying of Western education systems with little reference to Africa's educational needs obscures the developmental challenges of Africa. The study guidelines and case study examples are cited in many African universities based on European and USA standards. The university where I did my Honours in Town and Regional Planning is a good case. All the case studies were from Europe and the USA while I was studying. It is common in many African universities and high schools. However, in South Africa, where I did my master's, listening to your lecturer citing examples with local content and features was attractive. Citing local examples equips a student very well and makes learning more understandable.

Similarly, developing educational curriculums using local features and characters based on desired economic and social development will make learning easy and practice after graduation attractive. Barker (2017), citing Theresa May's speech on Brexit at Florence in September 2017, said, "Let us not seek merely to adopt a model already enjoyed by other countries. Instead, let us be creative and practical in designing an ambitious economic partnership that respects the freedoms and principles of the EU and the wishes of the British people". What does this speech teach us? It is to be innovative in our thinking and reasoning than copying others.

The role of education is to educate people on how to steer the economy in the direction the government wants the economy to grow. This is why Walter Rodney linked the colonial education of Africans to the economic gain of the colonial masters. Walter Rodney stated that the main drive of the colonial system was to train Africans to contribute to the domination and exploitation of the continent. He narrated that colonial education was subordination, exploitation, and conception of mental confusion for the benefit of the colonial masters. Hence, copying and perpetuating the same type of education as narrated by Rodney does not enhance the development of Africans but rather encourages the same mental confusion and economy sympathetic to the Western economy. Africa needs to be innovative in all aspects of development. They must develop unique social and economic theories and policies that suit the continent's conditions rather than copying ideas from other countries outside the mainland that do not suit Africa's challenges.

Africa needs an educational system where Western education models are reconciled with African culture and traditional methods. Nkrumah (1965) said, "While I fully subscribe to the vital principle of academic freedom, a university must relate its activities to the needs of the society in which it exists. In developing our universities, we must remember that once it had been planted in African soil, it must take root amidst African traditions and culture". This is because every society's cultural and traditional needs are unique. Society's issues and challenges might seem the same. However, each challenge and problem is unique, no matter how similar they might look. Hence, education must be channelled towards society's culture, tradition, and needs.

A flawed educational system is a mirror of weak leadership. When education fails, it breeds terrible leaders; when there are bad leaders, they are inconsiderate about the development of good-quality education. The only way to solve these challenges is to get the right people with correct thinking and proper education in power.

The lethargic attitude of leaders and political elites towards providing quality education in the continent significantly affects development. A passive attitude is what enhances fraud and corruption in the education system. Frauds include the unchecked character of teachers—lateness/tardiness to work, sexual abuse of students that goes unpunished, drug and alcohol intake during school hours, and avoiding classes. These forms of fraud, corruption, and teacher behaviour are due to leadership challenges.

In any society where corruption infiltrates the education system, development is derailed. A society with poor accountability in the education sector unleashes moral and value decay. When teachers are not accountable for their activities, the leaders are insensitive to children's and society's development. In some African universities, for a student to pass an exam or a subject, they must buy study material from a lecturer; if not, the lecturer intentionally fails them. It is common in some West African universities. Why must a student fail because of not buying a lecturer's study materials? If there is proper monitoring by the leadership and adequate procedure for accountability, the suffering of students at the hands of greedy and distorted lecturers and teachers will be reduced. When a student learns how to give bribes in school, when he becomes a leader, what would you expect from him or her? She or he will become an expert in enhancing corruption.

Corruption is destroying the fabric of the education sector. Often, money allocated for school infrastructure and facilities is misused and embezzled. In Limpopo Province, South Africa, books that were supposed to be delivered to students were dumped in unoccupied buildings. In many African countries, it can cost around 200,000 dollars by a private to build a private secondary school, while it will cost governments about 1.7 million dollars to build the same type of school.

Moletsi Mbeki said that South Africa has a fragile system of school accountability. He highlighted that there is strong support for teachers' development, but there needs to be a greater level of responsibility for performance. Moletsi Mbeki questioned why a black teacher in a township school should take their children and place them in a formerly white school miles away in a middle-class suburb. Then the same teacher disrupts the township school filled with children from poor communities during a public servants' strike, knowing that his or her own children are safely ensconced in a school where the timetable remains uninterrupted? Many public school teachers and lecturers send their children to private primary and secondary schools and universities in Nigeria. Then, these teachers and lecturers went on strike because of the lack of salary payments from the government, which affected learning for children from low-income households and poor homes. How do we expect good education when teachers are owed wages in months? Despite the challenges in providing adequate infrastructure and facilities in African schools, the ratio of the number of schools to the population is minimal. Similarly, many urban and rural schools need more desks, textbooks, stationery, and sanitation facilities.

Almost all the children of Nigerian leaders study in the best schools in Europe, Asia, South Africa, and the USA. Very few have their children in private schools in Nigeria, while Nigerian universities can go on strike for over seven months. Nigerian universities have lost up to three academic calendar years for the past 15 years. These leaders send their children to study outside of Africa because lecturers can go on strike for half of the year in Nigerian universities. How do we define impunity and rascality?

Ncana (2010) quoted Angelina Motshekga, the former Minister of Basic Education in South Africa, "We will not live up to our claim that every child is a national asset if we do not concentrate our efforts on tackling our immense infrastructural challenges". This statement highlights the grave challenges facing Africa's educational infrastructural development. The challenges are enormous. There needs to be more effort to solve the infrastructure development and facility delivery in African schools because of corruption and lack of transparency and accountability. In this modern and digital era, it is shocking that most African schools lack various educational facilities. Those in war-torn areas have no physical place to call their school, and many are afraid to go to school.

To draw attention to the poor state of infrastructural development in schools in Africa, particularly in universities, a feasibility report by Mohamoud (2005, p. 25) states:

> Poor infrastructure is a problem common to most African universities, as stated by the skilled African diaspora interviewed. Poor infrastructure manifests in dilapidated buildings, failing electricity, bad housing conditions and lack of proper services at university sites. Poor infrastructure is also a problem beyond university sites in many African cities, such as dilapidated and unpaved roads and inadequate transportation systems. Thus, poor infrastructure discourages the most highly skilled African diaspora from going to Africa and staying there for extended periods. However, for a temporary return, they are prepared, as one interviewee put it, 'to make a short professional sacrifice'.

Lack or shortage of basic facilities such as libraries, internet access, equipment, sports equipment, playgrounds, and laboratories are constraints existing in many universities. Furthermore, the lack or shortage of basic facilities is the primary reason that few students enrol in science and technology, and these are subjects where Africa needs expertise. However, the continent's economic crisis severely affects African higher education, creating a vicious cycle of development challenges.

There will be no miracle in African schools for better results when teachers need proper infrastructure. African universities are suffering from what could be called "education dehydration". South Africa could be exempted to an extent from the state of poor university infrastructure, but a few high institutions in South Africa still need an infrastructure upgrade. Many university students in West Africa need access to the internet provided by the universities. Their main entrance to the internet is through commercial internet cafés outside the school and students' personal cell phone networks. Many university lecturers cannot access the internet provided by the universities and computers. It is an era when university students in other continents have access to university and secondary school computers, tablets, and the internet, which makes learning easy. In 2015, the Gauteng Department of Education in South Africa started an incubation programme to use mobile tablets in teaching and learning for some schools. The idea was to enhance education, make learning easier, and allow students to adapt to the present computer and IT age. The pilot project by the Gauteng government since 2015 has not spread up to 30% of public schools in the province.

The challenges in education are immense because of the lack of comprehensive education policies that affect the standard of education. Where there are good policies, implementation is abysmal because of corruption and poor accountability. In some cases, education standards in secondary schools have been lowered to encourage a high pass rate. For example, in South Africa, some subjects have a pass mark of 30%. On the other hand, it does not encourage and prepare high school students for higher education. In 2017, the Nigerian government body responsible for conducting university entrance examinations reduced the cut-off point or pass mark to 120 out of 400. Lowering marks will not lead to economic production but might lead to high university dropouts. There are other forms of training, such as vocational training for skills development. Mass production of graduates by high institutions that need more quality education will enhance development.

5.2 Research

There needs to be a higher turnout of research in Africa. Low budgets and few research personnel in Africa affect research development and involvement. African leaders still need to fully comprehend the importance of research for development; hence, Africa's problems persist. Table 5.3 shows the commitment to research by selected African countries. The table was presented at an Intergovernmental Meeting on the African Observatory for Science, Technology and Innovation held on 9–11 May 2012, by Willie O. Siyanbola.

Table 5.3 highlights research challenges, which are the root of many of the continent's development issues. There needs to be more research development personnel and a research budget, as indicated in Table 5.3. Nigeria, with a population of 147,722 million, has research personnel per million inhabitants 222, while South Africa has 1207 personnel with a population of 49,173 million. Undesirable institutional conditions such as poor infrastructure and lack of funding impose substantial limitations on African research and research capacity building. Research is the basis of development. Without good research, achieving sustainable development will be a challenge. Networking and collaborations for research and development are vital. It encourages innovation and sustains technological and economic development.

African leaders act like the "Medical Newcomb's Problems". The "Medical Newcomb Problem" makes recommendations without knowing the problem's root. Newcomb's problems explain the reason for the decision of instability stated by Hansson (2003) in his story "Smoker's Dream". According to this story, the smoker dreams that there is no causal

Table 5.3 Capacity: Research and development personal and researchers

Countries	*R&D personnel*	*Researchers*	*Pop in millions*	*Research personnel per million inhabitants*	*Research per million inhabitants*
Cameron	5600	4562	18.660	300	244
Gabon	834	527	1.422	586	371
Ghana	2115	636	22.871	92	28
Kenya	6799	3794	37.755	180	100
Malawi	2884	733	14.846	194	49
Mali	2414	877	12.409	195	71
Mozambique	2082	522	21.869	95	24
Nigeria	32,802	17,624	147.722	222	119
Senegal	10,207	7859	11.893	858	661
South Africa	59,344	40,084	49.173	1207	815
Tanzania	3593	2755	41.276	87	67
Uganda	1768	785	30.638	58	26
Zambia	2219	612	12.314	180	50

Source: National Centre for Technology Management

connection between smoking and lung cancer. Instead, the observed correlation depends on gen, which causes lung cancer and smoking in its bearers. The smoker does not know if he has the gen in this dream. Suppose that he likes smoking but prefers being a non-smoker to taking the risk of contracting lung cancer. According to the expected utility theory, he should refrain from smoking. However, from a causal point of view, he should (in this dream of his) continue to smoke. "Smoker Dreamer" expresses a lack of scientific methodology in making decisions. The smoker relies on assumptions of whether to smoke or not to smoke. The "Medical Newcomb's Problem" is the dilemma of many African leaders. It explains why many leaders and political elites rely not on comprehensive research results but on personal assumptions and emotional decisions.

5.3 Labour

Labour is fundamental and essential for a successful life. There is only achievement and success with labour. When people dream and desire to have more, labour turns their dreams into reality. The journey of human civilisation highlights the significance of labour. Through labour, people transformed from the Stone Stage to the Computer State. Sometimes, work can be arduous and unpleasant, but the work must be turned in to guarantee success. There is no alternative to hard work; labour is vital to life. It is expected that leaders understand the role of labour in building industrial development and seize opportunities for the benefit of their countries. The ability to tap into the youth bulge of Asians has provided the labour needed to transform most Asian countries into exporters of manufactured goods. Chinese and Indians have capitalised on the population to give their nations an advantage in the production of industrial goods both for export and local markets. Europe and the USA developed because of African unpaid and cheap slave labour. The slave trade was inhumane and evil, but the USA and Europe utilised it for economic development. Then, in Africa, the population is acceptable. Even countries like Nigeria and Kenya still need to capitalise on it or take advantage of labour provided by their large populations for the agricultural and industrial revolution.

In Africa, leaders' visions have been blurred in exploiting population and natural resources for the benefit of industrialisation. A good combination of labour, abundant natural resources, and infrastructure development will guarantee that Africa will ensure sustainable growth. Africa should use its population size potential to produce cheaper quality goods. Moreover, Africa is well positioned concerning labour. Everyone has the talent to nurture and grow for social and economic benefits. Instead, there needs to be more dedication and energy to drive the development forward through the aggressive engagement of skills for labour. The situation has led to labour migration out of Africa. The present migration of workforce from Africa to Europe and the USA that keeps Western economies growing could be attributed to Africa's slow development pace. USA implemented the VISA Lottery Programme to attract labour for their economic development. Canada and Australia have visa-targeting skilled labour programmes for professionals, particularly African professionals with the best skills. The illegal and legal immigrants in Europe and the USA are skilfully exploited for their development. The reason behind this is labour.

Leaders and political elites' poor policy developments and strategic plans for economic growth are the outcomes of consistent and increasing labour migration out of Africa. Let me give a bit of personal analysis. The dreams of most graduates from high institutions from 1984 to 2010 were to travel, work and live in Europe, the USA, and Asia. Even those who travelled on visitor's visas during that period were sure not to return to

Nigeria. This applied to many West African countries. Fast forward to 2011 to 2014, some people who left for Europe, the USA, and Asia started returning to Nigeria for better life and work. Many Nigerians travelled to Europe, the USA, and Asia for tourism during the period. This is because of the better economic environment from 2010 to 2014 compared to 1984 to 2010. During 2010 and 2014, there was an increase in domestic and foreign investment. The economy was growing above 5%. The government created a conducive economic environment for investment. The situation changed in 2016, and Nigeria entered a recession. The economy shrank, and foreign investment reduced dramatically. In 2021 alone, more than sixty-eight thousand Nigerians moved to live in the UK alone.

The worst form of migration in the continent is migrating to Europe and the USA to provide cheap labour despite the professional certificate of the people involved in the shoddy work. It can be termed voluntary slavery. Voluntary slavery is because of increasing unemployment, political instability, and bad governance that led to mass migration. Voluntary slavery is a sign that leadership is failing to make productive engagement of its labour force. It creates loopholes that other continents exploit to source for their skilled and unskilled labour needs. The statement below throws light on the consequences of migration out of Africa:

> The flight of intellectual capital from Africa is alarming. The UN Economic Commission for Africa has estimated that between 1960 and 1975, 27,000 highly qualified Africans left the continent for the West. This number increased to approximately 40,000 between 1975 and 1984 and almost doubled by 1987, representing 30% of the highly skilled manpower stock—experienced personnel whom Africa can ill-afford to lose. Africa lost 60,000 professionals (doctors, university lecturers, engineers, scientists, etc.) between 1985 and 1990 and has been losing an average of 20,000 annually ever since. According to the International Organization for Migration (IOM), there are now 100,000 skilled Africans living and working in the EU and North America. To offset the severe skills shortage created by the lost human capital, African countries have recruited about 100,000 non-African skilled expatriates at an exorbitant cost, estimated at US$4 billion annually. There are currently only 20,000 scientists and engineers in Africa, serving a population of about 600 million. It is estimated that Africa would need at least 1 million scientists and engineers to meet and sustain its development goals. (Mohamoud 2005, p 8)

Information from the World Bank below further indicates how emigration has affected labour. World Bank Emigration information on Africa in 2009 shows that Africa had (Table 5.4):

1. Population: 840 million
2. The number of emigrants is 21.8 million.
3. The top ten countries that comprise the emigrants are Burkina Faso, Zimbabwe, Mozambique, Ivory Coast, Mali, Nigeria, Sudan, Eritrea, Democratic Republic of Congo, and South Africa

Emigration of Physicians (medical doctors and Nurses)
According to the World Bank Migration and Remittance Factbook (2011, Second Edition), it highlighted the following.

1. World Bank (2011b, p. 33) states that 21,516, or 18.4% of physicians trained in the region (World Bank quoted Bhargara, Docquier and Moullan 2011), emigrated.
2. World Bank (2011b, p. 33) stated that 36,653, or 28% of physicians trained in the region (Clemens and Pettersson 2006), emigrated.
3. World Bank (2011b, p. 33) stated that the emigration of nurses: 53,298 or 18% of nurses trained in sub-Saharan Africa.

While other continents are doing their best to keep their best brains, Africa is the opposite. Despite the numerous health challenges in Africa

Table 5.1 Skill emigration in 2000: Emigration rate of tertiary education population (Top ten countries)

Country	*Rate (%)*
Cape Verde	67.5
Gambia	63.5
Mauritius	56.2
Seychelles	55.9
Sierra Leone	52.5
Ghana	46.9
Mozambique	45.1
Liberia	45.0
Kenya	38.4
Uganda	35.6

Source: World Bank

and the need for health officials, Africa's skilled personnel keep migrating because of a lack of sound policies and poor development in various sectors. The statistics above are shocking. The emigration of highly skilled people from Africa has highlighted sustainable development challenges. A good leader will encourage job creation, innovations and, thereby, skills retention that reduce emigration; the lack of this in Africa has shown the leaders' nonchalant attitude towards skills retention and development. About 28% of trained physicians emigrated from Africa in 2006 and 18% of nurses in the same year, despite health challenges such as malaria, tuberculosis, and HIV.

I had an opportunity to interact with some doctors who work in the USA, Canada, and Europe through social media and telephone conversations. They indicated that their main reasons for emigrating from Africa were poor infrastructure and facilities in hospitals and lack of accountability and transparency by administrators of health systems, which frustrated their day-to-day functions. Some black doctors from other sub-regions, particularly West Africa and East Africa, who worked in Southern Africa before migrating to Europe, the USA, and Canada, complained about leaders' insensitivity to their welfare and poor policies for retention of black doctors who are not from Southern Africa.

The migration of physicians to other continents has reduced access to medical doctors, creating a huge health challenge in a continent where the population ratio to doctors is frightening. Table 5.5 shows the number of physicians per 10,000 population in some countries in Africa and other continents for comparison.

Table 5.5 shows the devastating effect of doctors' migration outside Africa. The ratio of one physician to a population of 10,000 calls for concern. How will the continent develop when labour is being weakened through migration, poor infrastructural development, lack of facilities, poor policy development, underutilisation of human resources, and abuse of labour rights? (Fig. 5.1).

The data above highlights the issues Africa faces despite the health challenges that need medical doctors' attention.

I have a friend who studied for a master's degree at a South African university; after some months of desperate job searching in South Africa without success, he moved to London, where he worked as a security guard. He had to move to the UK due to a desperate situation that allowed for cheap labour against the skilled contribution to African development. Why do African professionals migrate? What are the causes of their

Table 5.5 Number of physicians per 10,000 population in some selected African countries

Selected African countries in sub-Saharan Africa	*Number of physicians per 10,000*	*Comparison countries*	*Number of physicians per 10,000*
Nigeria	3.95	Brazil	25
South Africa	8.09		
Namibia	6.01	Singapore	24.34
Mauritius	26.58		
Botswana	3.48	Malaysia	22.28
Equatorial Guinea	3.5	Chile	29.73
DRC Congo	3.62	Ecuador	22.32
Sudan, Djibouti, Zambia, Guinea, and Kenya	Between 2–3	Cuba	84.27
Ivory Coast, Uganda, Zimbabwe, Ghana, Burkina, Cameroon, Mali, Rwanda, Ethiopia,	Between 1–2	China	23.87
Gambia, Somalia, Mozambique, Malawi, Niger, Sierra Leone, Liberia, Senegal, Tanzania, Burkina Faso, Benin, Chad	Between 0–1		

Source: WHO (2023)

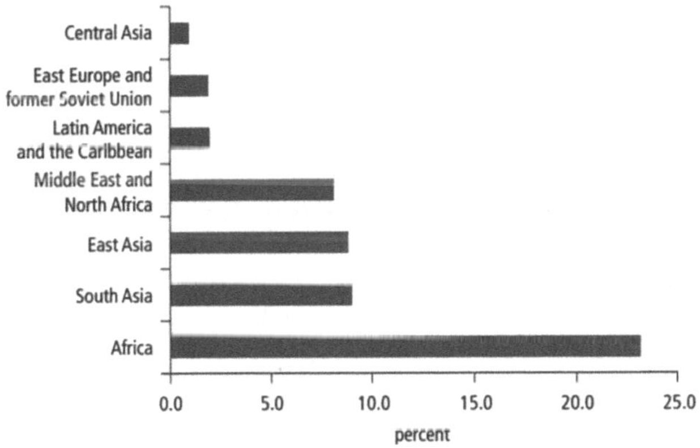

Fig. 5.1 Compares the migration of Africa-trained physicians to the rest of the continents. (Source: World Bank 2011)

migration? And finally, when they migrate, why do they not come back to Africa to share their gained knowledge for Africa's development? The migration of skilled professionals from Africa is a disadvantage to the continent, considering its numerous social and economic challenges. How long will the continent spend to educate its citizens while the West reaps the benefits of its efforts?

5.4 Experienced Studying in Africa

Coming from a middle-class Nigerian family in the 1970s to late 1990s, life was comfortable. The social and economic situation in Nigeria then was good. My father had extended family members who lived in our house, and their school fees were financed with the assistance of my parents. Before I could gain admission to the university in the early 1990s, the military leadership had collapsed the economy. The past army leaders who watched Nigeria's economy collapse were Yakubu Gowan, Murtala Ramat Mohammed, Olusegun Obasanjo, Mohammadu Buhari, Ibrahim Babangida, Sani Abacha, and Abdulsalami Abubakar.

To sustain the little pocket money from my parents for my daily upkeep at the university, I resorted to a feeding strategy called 0-1-0. (0-1-0 means that I don't eat in the morning; I eat around 3 pm and wait till the next day, and then drink water and take some form of local snacks popularly known as garri with groundnut or groundnut eaten with banana between 10 am and 12 noon and 5 pm and 10 pm. Sometimes, it would be 0-1-1; I don't eat in the morning but in the afternoon and evening. Some friends will offer me a third or second meal any day I am fortunate. I was under financial pressure and stress.)

After my university education, the Nigerian economy was stagnant despite the oil boom. There were high unemployment rates, and graduates could not get jobs; instead, they sat at home watching movies and going to pubs and restaurants to drink with little pocket money from their parents. There are policies called quota system (Some ethnic groups should be given preference in admission to universities because of their disadvantages in going to school and inability to get higher marks) and federal character (Ethnic groups should have equal access to employment and appointment) that were/are wreaking havoc on the merit needed to sustain the Nigeria economy. These policies were/are aimed at addressing the issues of ethnic representation in the public sector and admission to high institutions. The implication of these for admission into universities, recruitment into government offices and institutions, and promotion and appointment in government offices and institutions are based on these policies. These policies hinder any form of professionalism needed in delivering government responsibilities and accountability. These policies promote favouritism and nepotism, ethnicity and religion in recruitment, appointment, and promotion in working places. The policies encouraged mediocrity. For instance, if there are two Hausa employed, the next person to be used should be Yoruba or Igbo or any other ethnic group, whether they are qualified to execute the job responsibility. The policy wreaked havoc on the civil service. The policy is an instrument of tribalism in the public sector and government institutions. While some sections of Nigeria had to get jobs at government departments and institutions, others found it more accessible because of tribalism.

The quota system and federal character unleashed incompetency through university and secondary school education. For instance, the cut-off points to gain admission to study in the university or enter a secondary school education for students in specific areas remained high, while other regions enjoyed a shallow cut-off point. I was affected by the policy of a quota system in education based on different qualifying/cut-off points for other states in the same university in Nigeria. A discriminatory policy engineered by visionless leaders leads to development challenges.

Visualise this circumstance where your parents have financed you through university. They expected you to get a job after graduation and help in the family development or be self-independent. Their reward to finance your university education was their continued endeavours to shoulder your responsibilities after graduation. This is the situation most African graduates experience daily. This was my circumstance before I migrated to South Africa for further studies, hoping that after my master's education, I would be able to get a job in the growing South African economy. The considerable challenge I faced while studying in Nigeria did not offload itself, and it transformed into a different kind of challenge (financial hindrance). I had to hawk jewellery in offices in Durban to make a living and pay for my school fees. There needed to be more time for extracurricular activities.

One day, Professor Allison Todes, my lecturer at the University of KwaZulu Natal, who later became my dissertation supervisor, called me and said that the ideas and content of my schoolwork were perfect, but how I organised them could be better. "I have noticed that you don't edit your schoolwork before you hand it in". She hit the nail well but did not know what I was going through. She did not know that I had to pay for my own school fees, pay for where I am staying, feed myself and at the same time, go to classes on a full-time basis, do my assignments, including designs, and buy materials for my design assignments. Money for all these activities was from my hawking business.

There was neither time to rest nor to think; I was stressed physically and mentally. There is no room to edit my work and assignments and no time to reflect on my work. Every time, I was preoccupied with one activity or another just to survive. My worst nightmare was the little time I had for sleeping and resting. Some days, I did not sleep because of school assignments I had to complete. Each day, either I was hawking jewellery, running around to get money from customers who bought earrings on credit in class, listening to my lectures in the library, doing my assignments, or in the studio designing or busy with my domestic work. There was no time for entertainment, and thinking of entertainment was terrifying because of my personal economic situation and time.

Moreover, the student permit in South Africa allows students to engage in casual work, and the demand for casual work was low, and the payment could not sustain any foreign student who wanted to sponsor his/her education by doing such work. It was different from many African students who support their education through casual work in Europe and USA. Even when there was casual work, South African citizens were considered first, which was understandable because of the state of the economy and the growing unemployment.

There was a time when I had some savings from my income and used the money to call my friend who was studying in Europe, and he told me that he was working while studying part-time. He told me how he had sent money home for his siblings' school fees and for his father to buy a second-hand taxi for public transport to take care of the little household expenses. The challenges of African students are enormous. All my life in Africa has been about a struggle to keep myself in school and alive. The financial battle in the school impacted the quality of my schoolwork, not the content of my work, as pointed out by Professor Alison Todes, while my friend in Europe can make ends meet as a student. He had a work permit, while I did not have a work permit. He contributed to European economic growth, no matter how small. Then here I was, only struggling to survive.

It was an excruciating experience. Many Africans go to school daily in this same excruciatingly painful condition. This condition makes learning very difficult. Many African students could have made As and Bs in their exams and received first class from universities or high institutions of learning if they studied in the right conditions and circumstances. Colonialists perpetuated conditions that few African leaders fought and won on their Independence Day. Many African political leaders are perpetuating the same situation or worse than those perpetrated by the colonialists. These conditions are leadership-inflected because of corruption and poor governance.

The economic and political environment of the continent depicts the survival of those who have the mental strength to survive any economic and social conditions. Many African graduates are indebted by loans they borrowed or their parents borrowed to put them through university education and, simultaneously, face unemployment. It unleashes hard life on graduates who need access to jobs and funding for business. In Africa, particularly in Nigeria, some families sell properties to put their children through higher education institutions. These properties could have been a form of business rent or collateral for loans to start small-scale businesses. This environment hinders the survival spirit of growing youths and their ability to sustain themselves socially and economically.

CHAPTER 6

Economy and Agriculture

6.1 Natural Resources

Natural resources are the catalysts to a country's development when the benefits are used in diversifying the country's economy for social and economic growth. However, instead of natural resources catalysing social and economic development, they have become a curse in Africa. The curses of natural resources have divided communities, caused conflicts, source of corruption, and destruction of the livelihoods of communities. Table 6.1 highlights mineral resources found in each African country to understand how Africa is resourceful. The list needs to be completed.

Africa is endowed with many mineral deposits. Mining these mineral resources is relatively easy, but refining these minerals into finished goods is not. Why is it difficult to distil most of these natural resources to produce finished goods, creating jobs and enhancing economic development? For instance, Nigeria has oil and imports petrol and diesel, which cost the country millions of dollars daily. If these minerals are mined for the best interest of African countries, poverty will shrink, conflicts will be curtailed, people will be empowered, jobs will be created, infrastructure development will increase, and investment will swell. In addition, there will be a revolution in the industrial development of Africa.

Leadership mediocrity is the major challenge of the continent. Chinua Achebe (1984) called it the "occult of mediocrity" in his book titled *Trouble*

C. E. Osuigwe, *Leadership and Economic Development Challenges in Post-Colonial Africa*, Sustainable Development Goals Series,
https://doi.org/10.1007/978-3-031-45663-3_6

Table 6.1 Some of the natural resources in Africa

Country	*Natural resources*
Algeria	*Petroleum, Natural Gas, Iron Ore, Uranium, Lead, and Zinc*
Angola	*Petroleum, Diamond, Iron Ore, Phosphates, Copper, Feldspar, Bauxite, Uranium*
Benin	*Small Offshore Oil Deposit, Limestone, Marble, Timber*
Botswana	*Diamond, Copper, Nickel, Salt, Soda Ash, Potash, Coal, Iron Ore, Silver*
Burkina Faso	*Manganese, Limestone, Marble, Small Deposit of Gold, Phosphate Pumice, and Salt*
Burundi	*Nickel, Uranium, Rare Earth Oxides, Peat, Cobalt, Copper, Platinum, Vanadium, Arable Land, Niobium, Tantalum, Gold, Tin, Tungsten, Kaolin, Limestone, and Hydropower*
Cameroon	*Petroleum, Bauxite, Iron Ore, Timber, Hydropower*
Cape Verde	*Salt, Basalt Rock, Limestone, Kaolin, Fish, Clay, Gypsum*
Central African Republic	*Diamond, Uranium, Timber, Gold, Oil, Hydropower*
Chad	*Petroleum, Uranium, Natron, Kaolin, Gold, Limestone, Gravel, Salt*
Democratic Republic of Congo	*Cobalt, Copper, Niobium, Tantalum, Petroleum, Diamond, Gold, Silver, Zinc, Manganese, Tin, Uranium, Coal, Hydropower, Timber*
Congo Republic	*Petroleum, Timber, Potash, Lead, Zinc, Uranium, Copper, Phosphate, Gold, Magnesium, Natural Gas, Hydropower*
Cote d'Ivoire	*Petroleum, Natural Gas, Iron Ore, Diamond, Manganese, Cobalt, Bauxite, Copper, Gold, Nickel, Tantalum, Silica Sand, Clay, Hydropower*
Djibouti	*Geothermal, Gold, Clay, Granite, Limestone, Marble, Salt, Diatomite, Gypsum, Pumice, Petroleum*
Egypt	*Petroleum, Natural Gas, Iron Ore, Phosphate, Manganese, Limestone, Gypsum, Talc, Asbestos, Lead, Zinc*
Equatorial Guinea	*Petroleum, Natural Gas, Timber, Gold, Bauxite, Diamonds, Tantalum, Sand, Gravel, Clay*
Eritrea	*Potash, Gold, Zinc, Copper, Salt, Possibly Natural Gas, and Oil*
Ethiopia	*Small Reserve of Gold, Platinum, Copper, Potash, Natural Gas, Hydropower*
Gabon	*Petroleum, Natural Gas, Diamonds, Niobium, Manganese, Uranium, Gold, Timber, Iron Ore, Hydropower*
Gambia	*Titanium (Rutile and Ilmenite), Tin, Zircon, Silica Sand, Clay, Petroleum*
Ghana	*Gold, Timber, Industrial Diamonds, Bauxite, Manganese, Hydropower, Petroleum, Silver, Salt, and Limestone.*
Guinea	*Bauxite, Iron Ore, Diamond, Gold, Uranium, Hydropower, Salt*
Guinea-Bissau	*Timber, Phosphate, Bauxite, Clay, Granite, Limestone, Petroleum*

(*continued*)

Table 6.1 (continued)

Country	*Natural resources*
Kenya	*Limestone, Soda Ash, Salt, Gemstones, Fluorspar, Zinc, Diatomite, Gypsum, Wildlife, Hydropower*
Lesotho	*Water, Diamonds, Sand, Building Stone, Clay*
Liberia	*Iron Ore, Timber, Diamonds, Gold, Hydropower*
Libya	*Petroleum, Natural Gas, Gypsum*
Madagascar	*Graphite, Chromite, Coal, Bauxite, Salt, Quartz, Tar Sands, Semiprecious Stones, Mica, Hydropower*
Malawi	*Limestone, Hydropower, Uranium, Coal, Bauxite*
Mali	*Gold, Phosphate, Kaolin, Salt, Limestone, Uranium, Coal, Bauxite*
Mauritania	*Iron Ore, Gypsum, Copper, Phosphate, Diamond, Gold, Oil*
Morocco	*Phosphate, Iron Ore, Manganese, Lead, Zinc*
Mozambique	*Coal, Titanium, Natural Gas, Hydropower, Tantalum, Graphite*
Namibia	*Diamond, Copper, Uranium, Gold, Silver, Lead, Tin, Lithium, Tungsten, Zinc, Salt, Hydropower, Coal, Oil, Iron Ore*
Niger	*Uranium, Coal, Iron Ore, Tin, Phosphate, Gold, Molybdenum, Salt, Petroleum*
Nigeria	*Natural Gas, Petroleum, Tin, Iron Ore, Coal, Limestone, Niobium, Lead, Zinc*
Rwanda	*Gold, Cassiterite (Tin Ore), Wolframite (Tungsten Ore), Methane, Hydropower*
São Tomé and Príncipe	*Hydropower*
Senegal	*Phosphate and Iron Ore*
Seychelles	*Copra*
Sierra Leone	*Diamond, Titanium Ore, Bauxite, Iron Ore, Gold Chromite*
Somalia	*Uranium, Iron Ore, Tin, Gypsum, Bauxite, Copper, Vanadium, Salt, Natural Gas*
South Africa	*Gold, Chromium, Antimony, Coal, Iron Ore, Manganese, Nickel, Phosphate, Tin, Uranium, Diamonds, Platinum, Copper, Vanadium, Salt, Natural Gas*
Sudan and South Sudan	*Petroleum, Iron Ore, Copper, Chromium Ore, Zinc, Tungsten, Mica, Silver, Gold, Hydropower*
Swaziland	*Asbestos, Coal, Clay, Cassiterite, Hydropower, a Small Quantity of Gold and Diamond*
Tanzania	*Tanzanite, Gemstone, Hydropower, Tin, Phosphate, Iron Ore, Coal, Diamond, Gold, Natural Gas, Nickel*
Togo	*Phosphate, Limestone, Marble*
Tunisia	*Petroleum, Phosphate, Iron Ore, Lead, Zinc, Salt*
Uganda	*Copper, Cobalt, Hydropower, Limestone, Salt, Gold*
Zambia	*Copper, Cobalt, Zinc, Lead, Coal, Emeralds, Gold, Silver, Uranium, Hydropower*

(*continued*)

Table 6.1 (continued)

Country	*Natural resources*
Zimbabwe	*Coal, Chromium Ore, Asbestos, Gold, Nickel, Copper, Iron Ore, Vanadium, Lithium, Tin, and Platinum.*

Source: The world factbook, investment and promotion agencies

Note: There are some changes made on the table

with Nigeria. The occult of mediocrity explains the impact of mediocrity on social and economic development due to weak leadership. Klein (2007), in her book *The Shock Doctrine*, said that in Nigeria, 70% of Nigerians still survive with less than $1 a day while Shell still makes super profits. Not only does Shell make tremendous profits in Nigeria's oil fields, but many other oil companies are fraudulently taking advantage of weak political leadership in Nigeria with corrupt political elites. Equatorial Guinea, which has a major oil deal with Exxon Mobil, got to keep a mere 12% of the oil revenues in the first year of its contract, a share so low it would have been scandalous even at the height of colonial oil pillage (CBS news programme 60 minutes). Consistent failure in harnessing natural resources for the benefit and development of Africa hangs on the shoulders of the political elites and leaders, and it is an embarrassment and a scandal to Africa's image.

6.2 African Markets

The importance of substantial African markets is witnessed at the rate Asians, Americans, and Europeans are scrambling to tap into the markets with their manufactured goods and services. The reason is that Africa needs to produce more to supply its growing population.

The African middle class are beckoning on what other nations produce because they are young and upwardly mobile. Nevertheless, there are exceptions in specific industries, such as Nigeria's Nollywood entertainment, which is doing well in Europe, Asia, and the USA. Likewise, African music, particularly in Nigeria and South African music industries, is acceptable worldwide. Nigerian musicians are among the best in the world and are sought after by the entertainment industry. There is a rise in African fashion and designers; many have used the West African fabric called Ankara as a mode of design to capture the world's attention. The Kenyan flower industry is doing well, and so are the shoe and textile industries in

Ethiopia, and former Nigerian textile industries are trying to come back to life. These developments are because of individual drive and efforts rather than government policies and motivations. Regardless of the exceptions mentioned above, there is a challenge in developing comprehensive policies for the integration of the African market. Limitations in the integration of the African market are linked to untargeted policies and inadequate inclusive strategies, as well as conflicts and poor infrastructural development.

In some countries such as South Africa, Lesotho, Swaziland, Namibia, and Botswana, indigenous African food is phasing out in the marketplaces and household cookeries. The consumption of African food within these countries is lower than what is expected. It could be ascribed to limitations on the production or poor strategies and policies to enhance indigenous African food crop production and marketing. A few restaurants sell traditional African cuisines. In a region where almost 80% of the population is black, it is expected that the thriving restaurants should be the ones that define the culture of the people, but the case is the opposite. The role played by the apartheid system in eroding the African indigenous foods is understandable; there should be government initiatives to encourage investment in restaurants that promote indigenous Southern African staples, thereby encouraging indigenous crop production and empowering rural farmers.

Similarly, for decades, Africa has depended on Western institutions and individuals regarding the economy of trade intermediaries for goods and services. Presently, there is a shift to Asia for such services. The challenges of trade intermediaries create an unsustainable "middleman" market in the continent. An intermediary facilitates negotiations between manufacturers and retailers, sometimes directly with consumers. Africans must fully participate in commercial intelligence that informs the intermediary's job in the global value chain. Poor participation in commercial intelligence could be traced to poor industrial growth, poor services, awareness, and inefficient negotiation skills needed internationally. Other forms of trade intermediaries' constraints in Africa include—political instability, unpredictable accurate exchange rates, lack of capital depth, institutional weakness, and limited market intelligence, among others.

In addition, e-commerce, which is defining the new world in wholesale and retail trade, has yet to be fully embraced by Africans. Amazon from USA, and Alibaba is from Asia; these two are among the biggest in e-commerce. Others like eBay and Google are competing in the wholesale market and shaping the world of trade and marketing. There might be virtual shopping malls where people will stay in the comfort of their homes and buy things in a virtual mall. Where is Africa in this context? Africans are innovative, and they try their best without government support. However, the social and economic environment and poor governance do not allow the youth to apply their minds developmentally.

6.3 Agriculture

Agriculture is the backbone of the economy of any country. Agricultural development provides food, raw materials, and employment opportunities to a large percentage of a country's population. The development of agriculture leads to the construction of irrigation schemes, drainage systems, and other agriculture-related infrastructure. Similarly, the primary source of national income for many African countries is subsistence farming and agriculture. From the pre-colonial period, fair trade was exchanged among the kingdoms in Africa. In the first decade after independence, many African countries exported agricultural goods to Western countries and had food security. After more than four decades of independence of most African countries, it is expected that African countries should be one of the continents feeding the world, but the world is providing the continent through food aid. "The State of New Poverty Narrative", a report by Kharas et al. (2018) on the Brookings Institution website, states:

> According to our projections, Nigeria has already overtaken India as the country with the largest number of extreme poor in early 2018, and the Democratic Republic of the Congo could soon take over the number 2 spot (Figure 1 below). At the end of May 2018, our trajectories suggest that Nigeria had about 87 million people in extreme poverty, compared with India's 73 million. What is more, extreme poverty in Nigeria is growing by six people every minute, while poverty in India continues to fall. Already, Africans account for about two-thirds of the world's extreme poor. If current trends persist, they will account for nine-tenths by 2030. Fourteen out of 18 countries in the world—where the number of extreme poor is rising—are in Africa.

What went wrong? Mbeki (2011) said that today, Africa is primarily hungry, and it is the most food-insecure continent in the world, thus causing a reduction in productivity and growth. For instance, Malaysia came to Nigeria to obtain palm oil seeds in the 1960s for agricultural production. By 1990, Malaysia was exporting more palm oil products than Nigeria.

The continent's agricultural bases are in the rural areas, and access to the market keeps the rural farmers less profitable and limits production. Rural farmers' limitation to markets is the result of bad leadership that needs to be developing rural transportation systems, infrastructure, information systems, and internet access. May (2000) said that efficient and reliable transport addresses the issue of isolation and widens access to the centre of economic activities and income generation. He highlighted that increasing people's capacity to travel also opens opportunities to boost their knowledge and education, encourages and broadens the scope within which the poor can seek support and develop aid, and easy ways to deliver goods and services.

The resilience of African women and rural farmers is feeding the African population. Most of the efforts have been made without assistance from the leaders or government policies. However, there might be exceptions. For instance, former president Goodluck Jonathan introduced an electronic transfer programme named e-wallet for farmers in Nigeria. Under this agricultural development programme, rural farmers were empowered, and food security in Nigeria improved and contributed more than 10% to the Nigerian GDP from 2012 to 2014. When President Muhammadu Buhari came to power in 2015, he suspended the programme, leading to increased poverty in Nigeria and bad governance and corruption.

In West Africa, there is a massive market for indigenous agricultural produce. All over the world, Nigerian or West African food products and spices can be found. The sustainability of indigenous food production by Nigerians and West Africans is mainly due to their attitude towards their indigenous food. They prefer West African food to any other type of food. The behaviour has helped sustain local subsistence agriculture and reduced poverty in West Africa, particularly in Nigeria. As mentioned earlier, this is an individual commitment and community effort. Despite the progress in indigenous West African food production, there are challenges facing rural farmers. The challenges include poor infrastructural development (roads, electricity, and water), lack of agricultural facilities, inadequate government assistance to farmers, lack of access to capital to revolutionise and innovate indigenous agricultural production, and limitations to e-commerce. Other challenges include a lack of support through targeted government policies and inclusive strategies, and where there are good policies and procedures, lack of transparency and accountability by the leadership derails the purpose.

Western countries have not dominated indigenous West African food production and marketing, as they have succeeded in the Southern African market. The distortion of Southern African indigenous food production could be traced to the apartheid government. They can revisit their indigenous agricultural output with the current land reform programme, benefitting small-scale farmers producing indigenous crops for local and international consumption. The Southern Africans must emulate the Indians. For more than a century, the Indians and Chinese have stayed and worked in South Africa, and they treasure the culture they are used to. They import their food and spices from Asia. In most cities in Southern Africa, it is easy to find Indian spice shops and restaurants and Chinese restaurants, but hard to find restaurants serving indigenous Southern African foods. The same mentality keeps the Indians and Chinese in Asia fast-tracking their development.

Presently, the biggest challenge to agricultural development in Africa is foreigners scrambling for African land and governments selling off African land. To an African, land ownership means pride, and land ensures the connectivity of the ancestors' property to the living. Many African tribes, by culture and nature, do not sell land but can lend land to another person and get it back at a stipulated time without asking for money or looking for interest from the borrower. To all Africans, life revolves around land. Despite all these, the recent scramble for land by foreigners in Africa has gained momentum.

What necessitates land scramble by foreigners is the untapped nature of African land. The land scramble perpetuates social pain and economic hardship in African communities. It disempowers the poor and middle-income groups while increasing unemployment, mainly in rural communities. Selling land through what the government terms foreign investment indicates a need for more vision for development. At the World Summit on Food and Security at Room in 2009, the Food and Agriculture Organization of the United Nations reported that the extent of land in Africa acquired by foreign interests in the last three years is projected to be up to 20 million hectares. The purpose of foreign land acquisition in Africa is to secure the food security of their countries, which will have a devastating effect on food security in Africa. If the momentum of acquiring land continues, rural people's access to land will be easier in many countries, and the outcome will damage sustainable food production. However,

Africa needs foreign investment, but not to the detriment of poverty alleviation through access to land. To Africans, the land is the source of sustainable livelihood.

The increase in land scramble has not gone unnoticed, causing irritation in some areas. This, however, has continued African leaders to carry out their intended acts of selling off agricultural lands. Some leaders stopped selling farmlands after protests from rural farming communities. For example, the former president of Senegal (Abdoulaye Wade) froze such an investment when Senegalese protested against foreign firms using 20,000 hectares of land for bio-fuel farm production. While in some African countries, such deals could have been successful despite their social and economic consequences, even though rural farmers rely on farming as their only means of production and survival.

Plaizier (2016) said there is vast room for improvement, and Africa remains a net food importer, although it has 60% of the world's uncultivated arable land. Plaizier further highlighted that as its population has doubled and tripled in urban areas in the past 30 years, agricultural production and food security have resisted keeping pace. This fact makes the continent vulnerable to land scramble for international efforts to feed the planet's growing population, and African leaders need help using vast arable land in the continent.

6.4 Capitalism and Entrepreneurship

After independence, many African countries implemented a capitalist economic approach, while some implemented communism. Presently, the economies of almost all African countries are associated with capitalism. In Africa, capitalism has taken the form of what could be termed rental capitalism (natural resources capitalism). In Nigeria, this can be referred to as petroleum/contract capitalism; in South Africa, it is tender/mineral resources capitalism. Technology innovation and development in the West sustain the Western capitalist approach to economic growth, while aggressive manufacturing is growing Asian economies. Due to the nature of capitalism in Africa, many capitalists seek little means of production and economic development that are not mining and contracts. Nigeria's government spent over 3 billion dollars looking for oil exploration in Northern Nigeria. The money can boost Northern Nigeria's agricultural potential and create more jobs than oil production.

When most of the capitalists in Africa make billions through natural resources, contracts, and tenders with little emphasis on other forms of production, it affects sustainable development. It is because mineral resources, tender and contract capitalists are based on connection to corrupt leaders and political elites rather than hard work. When the ties to leaders and political elites are no more, the businesses fail because of the unsustainable way some capitalists do business. These capitalists find it challenging to transform from mineral resources, tender, and contract capitalists to build a sustainable manufacturing, technological innovation, and development business that will last for decades and centuries. For example, establishing companies that provide a spectrum of services to other forms of institutions that are not public sector, creating business and product brands that will capture a broad range of consumers and clients, and developing brands that attract clients rather than connections and network with government and leaders and political elites. There are exceptions, but the level of engagement is very minimal. For instance, many world-known brands started over a century ago and dominate the world economy. How many African brands can reach the world except for a few companies from South Africa?

African capitalism's challenges are affected mainly by how banks and financial institutions grant loans to small businesses. In Nigeria, the lending rate of banks is at least 18% for a short repayment period of five years for most small businesses. How could a company survive in such a situation? However, banks in Nigeria cannot say with certainty an individual's residence or place of origin. There needs to be a system where organisations can check an individual's financial history or credit records. This is common in many African countries. There needs to be more demographic data or information that can be used for security checks. It shows failed leadership and affects banks' confidence in granting loans to small businesses.

Similarly, the number of entrepreneurial developments in Africa is "pint-sized" compared to the continent's population and social and economic potential to sustain a capitalist state. Understandably, entrepreneurship is an individual effort but should be reinforced by government policies and strategies. Because of a lack of government support, many entrepreneurs are involved in importing finished goods and services. These forms of entrepreneurship do not enhance employment opportunities and are detrimental to industrial development. Many entrepreneurs are interested in importation because of poor infrastructural development, particularly electricity and water. A country like Nigeria that cannot provide constant electricity should expect something other than industrialisation but the importation of goods and services. The consistent load-shedding in the South from 2021 to the present has affected many businesses, particularly small businesses that could not afford electricity. How can a country develop without a sound and sustainable infrastructure?

In 2011, at a breakfast function to celebrate the South African Institute of Chartered Accountants (SAICA) progress in its Black Entrepreneurship Initiative (BEI), Nonkululeko Gobodo warned South African entrepreneurs that they are emerging from a past without opportunities. Now, they have all these opportunities, and she finds it so sad that they waste them by chasing money instead of advancing sustainable businesses. She said that life is a journey by itself, and part of it is developing a business. When one chases money hurriedly, one will lose it. She argued that one might have a contact at a government department pumping tenders to one. If that person resigns, one might lose one's lifestyle, which one was used to, and it might be challenging to make a comeback. She advised that they should focus on building a sustainable business that will be there in five or ten years, but they need a career in tenders. An individual's lifestyle and lack of mentorship are challenges to building sustainable economic growth.

Leaders have developed policies and programmes for SMMEs in a little effort to encourage entrepreneurship. Many of these programmes have not been sustainable and failed because of poor implementation, corruption, and lack of accountability. The successful implementations of SMME programmes have been derailed because of leadership interference. Political appointees who manage these SMME programmes have yet to gain professional knowledge of local economic development, financial or micro-economic development or management. Sometimes, appointments are carried out based on ethnic bias and political alliance. There is a need for professionalism and skills to drive successful SMMEs, which deters the potential use of opportunities for creating employment and alleviating poverty.

The nature of capital is like a chameleon; it changes colours based on the behaviours of the leaders. It changes with the attitude of leaders. It has so much emotion. It depends on how you develop, implement, and manage capital. The behaviour of African leaders frightens financial capital because it moves to where it feels comfortable. Sustainable financial wealth does not like conflicts, corruption, and fraud. Money hates mismanagement, lack of accountability, and transparency. The nature of financial capital and investment in Africa is complex, and it is a challenge to sustainable entrepreneurship development.

CHAPTER 7

Infrastructure

7.1 Pitiable Infrastructure Development

For a country to grow sustainably, investment in infrastructure should be a key priority. The challenges in Africa are primarily linked to poor infrastructure development and poor drive-in infrastructure investment. Africa Development Bank (AFDB) (2013), in their report "An Integrated Approach to Infrastructure Provision in Africa", highlighted the following:

1. Naidoo (2023) quoted the South Africa Reserve Bank that the electricity crisis in South Africa is costing the country as much as 899 million rand ($49 million) per day and will trim 2 percentage points off output growth in 2023, according to South African Reserve Bank estimates. The state of South Africa's electricity blackout is minimal compared to Nigeria, where electricity can go off for two to one week, and the dire consequences to Nigeria's social and economic growth. And this is a common scenario in many African countries.
2. A regional and multipurpose approach in the water sector constitutes a promising way forward. Although Africa enjoys about 5.4 trillion cubic meters of plentiful water resources annually, it needs to harness water for development. Just 3.8% of this figure has so far been developed, and 300 million Africans still need access to

C. E. Osuigwe, *Leadership and Economic Development Challenges in Post-Colonial Africa*, Sustainable Development Goals Series,
https://doi.org/10.1007/978-3-031-45663-3_7

safe drinking water. In addition, less than 5% of agricultural land is irrigated, and less than 10% of hydropower potential is captured.

3. More than 640 million Africans have no access to energy, giving an electricity access rate for African countries at just over 40%—the world's lowest; across Africa in 2014, average electricity access was about 72% in urban areas, more than double that of rural Africa's 33% (AFDB 2018). In sub-Saharan Africa, only 24% of the population have access to safe drinking water, and 28% have basic sanitation facilities that are not shared with other households (UN 2019).
4. Mitchell (2021) states that 28% of the population of sub-Saharan Africa had mobile internet connectivity in 2020 compared with 49% of people globally, as reported by GSMA, a research company, and around 300 million people in sub-Saharan Africa had connectivity to the internet via their mobile phones in 2020, up from 120 million people or 13% of the population in 2014. Mitchell further indicated that in 2018, 19% of people lived in areas not covered by mobile networks, and an additional 53% did not use mobile internet despite having coverage. This is an era when digital marketing has become a source of improving economic growth and access to economic opportunities.

Let's look at the comparison of electricity production in different continents (Fig. 7.1).

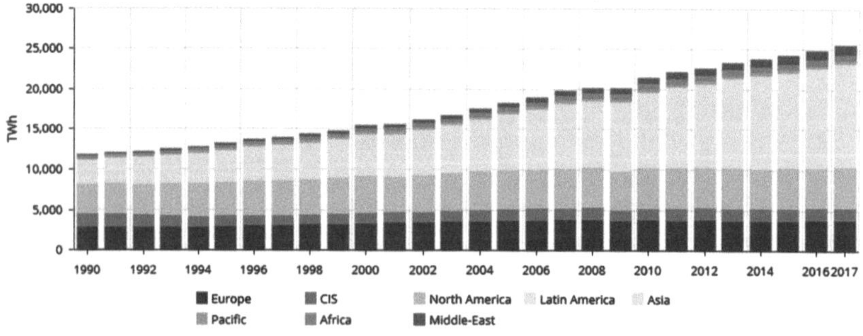

Fig. 7.1 Electricity production continent comparison. (Source: Global Energy Statistical Yearbook 2018)

According to the information from the Global Energy Statistical Yearbook 2018, the production of electricity between 2010 and 2017 is indicated below in Terawatt per hour (TWH).

Table 7.1 shows that Africa produces less electricity when compared to other continents. The report states that Europe per TWH is 3886, North America is 4963, Latin America is 1590, the Middle East is 1190, and Asia is 11,274. The report further explained that India, Japan, and China accounted for ¾ of the global electricity rise in 2017. Before 2003, North America produced more electricity than Asia; by 2004, Asia started producing more than North America as their industrial power increased. During the same period, Africa's electricity production remains pathetic. In Nigeria, most of its cities and towns cannot have constant electricity for three successful days; many cities or towns cannot have continuous electricity in a day. Many rural areas are not connected to electricity.

UNSAID (----) reported that Nigeria is the largest economy in sub-Saharan Africa, but limitations in the power sector constrain growth. Nigeria is endowed with large oil, gas, hydro and solar resource, and it already has the potential to generate 12,522 megawatts (MW) of electric power from existing plants, but most days is only able to generate around 4000 MW, which is insufficient. According to the Ministry of Energy, South Africa's total domestic electricity generation capacity is 58,095 megawatts (MW) from all sources. Approximately 91.2%, or 46,776 MW, comes from thermal power stations, while 4533 MW, or 8.8%, is generated from renewable energy sources. Africa has abundant coal, rivers, and enough sunlight for solar power; what is then deterring African leaders

Table 7.1 Electricity production in Africa compared to Asia

Year	*Africa*	*Asia*
2010	675	7983
2011	699	8581
2012	727	8958
2013	747	9539
2014	772	9934
2015	790	10,226
2016	801	10,691
2017	801	11,274

Source: Global Energy Statistical Yearbook 2018

from making proper plans for energy production for industrial development and economic growth? Is Asia not colonised as well as Africa? The leadership's determination and focus on developing the continent is the answer. Africa Development Bank has numerous good recommendations for tackling Africa's infrastructure challenges, particularly in their report, "An Integrated Approach to Infrastructure Provision in Africa (2013)". Why is the implementation poor? Many leaders intentionally have mental blockades in the continent while companies rob their citizens of their hard-earned money for selfish interests. It is a place where people pay for very low-quality services at exorbitant prices. A good case is Nigeria's power supply, where a citizen can pay an electricity bill without experiencing a power supply for up to 15 days a month.

Some of the railway lines used when the colonialists left Africa 40 years ago have ceased functioning; some that are working must be fixed to the expected capacity. I have crisscrossed South Africa and seen many abandoned railway lines, and I beg the question, why? From the 1960s to 1980 in Nigeria, railway lines connected the Eastern to the Northern and Western to the North and were functioning at total capacity and creating thousands of jobs, allowing the free flow of goods from the rural areas to the urban centres. The services made life easier for poor travellers who could not afford to pay taxi or bus transport fares. From 1980 until 2010, two decades later, the railway lines ceased to operate, and thousands of employees lost their jobs, leading thousands, if not millions, into poverty. It was only in 2012 that the president of Nigeria started reviving the dead railway transport system. The economic consequences of these three decades in which the railways failed to operate can be measured in billions of dollars. "One of the greatest scandals after decades of underinvestment in Africa is the state of the continent's transportation infrastructure. Virtually, all the railway lines that were in use when the colonialists left sub-Saharan Africa between 40 and 50 years ago have long ceased to operate or are operating at a fraction of their design capacity", said M. Mbeki (2009, p. 30). Mbeki called it "scandals" as it is a high level of human abuse. It is expected that by now, the railway system development could have developed faster than it was 50 years ago. The African leadership could have added or built more railway lines. Africa could have moved to faster railway services in Europe or Asia. Instead, we have seen a decline or ceased operations from what was started more than 50 years ago by the colonialists and leaders of the early days of independence. If the leaders were focused and accurate to the continent's vision, railway lines could have been crisscrossing communities and the whole continent, thereby reducing the burden of transport fares. It could have increased rural-urban transportation of agricultural produce that sustains rural dwellers and women responsible for the continent's economic development challenges.

The worst era in Nigeria was between 1983 and 1999. Roads became death traps, the health system collapsed, and school buildings and facilities dilapidated. I spent most of my childhood in a rural area. I remember vividly as a kid that in the 1980s, there were public water taps in rural communities and households that could afford the connection. Tap water ran daily, if not at least four times a week. My father had a water tap in our house. By the end of the 1980s, tap water had ceased running until now. In a high-level meeting on Africa's development needs, the United Nations in New York on 22 September 2008 stated that hundreds of millions of Africans lack even the most fundamental amenities, particularly in rural areas, where most of the continent's 920 million people live. It further stated that the burden falls most heavily on women, who spend hours collecting wood for cooking and heating without electricity, and rural women who walk an average of six kilometres daily to rivers and springs due to lack of piped water.

Economists refer to infrastructure as an overhead resource and capital in development. Infrastructure enhances productivity and the potential ability of human capital and growth. Lack of infrastructure leads to a lack of human development and retards human capacity. The call for infrastructural development seems to fall on deaf ears of many leaders who pay little attention to infrastructural development. Infrastructure such as electricity supplies, roads, ports, and telecommunication includes services and intermediary goods needed to develop public and private sector productivity. Nigeria has the capacity of at least four international standard seaports, but it has only one serious functioning seaport in Lagos, while South Africa has more than five good functioning seaports. Table 7.2 highlights the population of Africa to significant infrastructural development.

Africa's access to roads and electricity per population is 43% below an average of 50%. Every aspect of infrastructural accessibility is below average except for mobility accessibility and water. Africa performed poorly compared to the rest of the developing countries in the world. The state of poor infrastructure development is mainly a result of leaders' neglect and corruption. The imbalance created by the West for many years might take years to amend and balance. Nevertheless, it is frustrating that many

Table 7.2 Infrastructure per population

Item	*All African countries*	*Africa's poorest countries*	*Developing countries*	*World*
Electricity coverage, % of population	43%	31%	77%	82%
Access to all-season roads, % of rural population	43%	35%	67%	69%
Mobile penetration rate, % of population	80%	–	89%	96%
Improved water, % of population	68%	59%	87%	89%
Improved sanitation, % of population	40%	28%	57%	64%
People living in slum conditions, % of the population	50%	–	33%	–

Source: Africa Development Bank, World Bank Group, International Energy Agency, International Telecommunication Union, TA Telecom, World Health Organization, United Nations Children's Fund, and United Nations Department of Economic and Social Affairs

leaders still need to develop comprehensive strategies and policies for correcting the imbalance.

A study by the Africa Development Bank, AFDB (2018) indicates that new estimates suggest that the continent's infrastructure needs amount to $130–170 billion a year, with a financing gap in the range of $68–$108 billion. However, Boko (2018) states that illicit financial flows impede Africa's development, and Boko further highlighted that "it is estimated that $100 billion a year, about four per cent of Africa's GDP, have been illegally earned, transferred, or used, much of it due to miss-invoicing. This retards Africa's growth; weakens public institutions and the rule of law; discourages the culture of paying taxes and value-addition to natural resources; and results in countries' over-reliance on official development assistance". The money illegally could have helped to bridge the gap in infrastructure development.

During colonial rule, infrastructure delivery was developed through class and race. Infrastructure delivery during the colonial era affected African development. However, most African countries' current unhurried infrastructure development reflects ethnic favouritism and political alliances used during the colonial period. There have been instances where leaders locate projects in an area where the cost of development and possible maintenance is higher when compared to a more feasible location within the same state, province, or country because of regional politics. Some bigoted leaders in Africa embarked on incapacitating ethnic groups through infrastructure delivery. Many times, a region or ethnic group is neglected in the delivery of infrastructure such as water, sanitation, hospitals, electricity, education, and communication. Allocation of infrastructure according to ethnic groups perpetuates inequalities within ethnic groups and affects their income. It also diminishes the standard of living of the ethnic group whom the denial of infrastructure delivery is perpetrated against.

Many African leaders and political elites spend billions of dollars in health tourism each year in Europe, Asia, and the USA because of poor health infrastructure in the countries they lead. Travelling outside the continent for health tourism is sponsored by tax money. On the other hand, the general citizens need access to better education and health, and many die because of a lack of basic healthcare facilities. Many children have dropped out of school because they must walk more than five kilometres daily to go to school while their leaders use their resources to access the best infrastructure in other countries outside Africa, which also aids in leakages of money from the continent.

Creating reputable names in Africa is not a wish for many companies' owners or shareholders. This is because of their linkage and relationship to leaders and political elites. In Nigeria, for instance, from the 1980s to 2022, local governments and state roads do not last more than two years, and they will be in bad condition with potholes. This does not stop leaders from awarding the same companies contracts. In all parts of Africa, you see companies that did a terrible job winning government contracts. We need to ask what is wrong with the system. Is it that the head is rotten, or the tail is confused? Blacklisting bad companies does not stop them from getting jobs or contracts. Despite multinational and domestic companies' bad reputations for delivering low-quality work in Africa, these companies continue to thrive. This emphasises that connections to African leaders and political elites guarantee winning contracts and tenders. It directly affects sustainable infrastructural development and economic growth.

In Nigeria, for instance, it is unsurprising that some roads have been reconstructed more than five times in ten years. The reconstruction of these roads was because of their substandard nature. Ex-governor of Imo State Rochas Okorocha once blamed acid rain for the damages to new roads he constructed. You ask yourself, when did acid start to rain from the sky in Imo State. The worrying aspects of the reconstruction of the new road are the wasteful expenditure and hindrance to the easy flow of goods and people. There are many instances in the West where firms and companies lost clients and folded because they lost credibility and were dishonest in delivering their duties.

A good example is Arthur Anderson in the Enron scandal of 2002. The untold stories of multinational companies operating in Africa and their impact on the development of Africa are well known. Despite their bad reputations, African leaders and political elites turn a blind eye to their social and economic damage to society and communities.

CHAPTER 8

Corruption and Underdevelopment in Africa

8.1 Corruption and the Leadership

Corruption in Africa had its roots in the exploitation by colonial rule. During the colonial era, Africans were taught how to exploit their people. For example, the use of warrant chiefs by the British to exploit the Igbos through fraudulent taxation. To the point that warrant chiefs became lords and recklessly seized people's properties. An Igbo proverb says, "It is the rat at home that tells the bush rat that there is meat or fish in the oven or cupboard". The Igbo proverb expresses the corrupt relationship between the West/Asia and African countries. Similarly, a Chinese proverb says, "A fish always starts rotting from the head". When a leader is corrupt, his subordinates can easily be corrupted. This proverb relates to an English adage that says, "The rotten apple injures its neighbour". One person's corruption in a government quickly corrupts other fellows. Corruption is one of the biggest impediments obstructing African citizens from realising their visions. It distorts a comprehensive economic environment for entrepreneurial growth. Corruption does not allow good policies to be implemented or to enhance a vibrant economic environment. Corruption allows a sanctuary for the selfish accumulation of wealth at a vast cost to hapless citizens. It kills more than conflicts and wars. Corruption leads to bad service delivery and lousy health care. Africans

C. E. Osuigwe, *Leadership and Economic Development Challenges in Post-Colonial Africa*, Sustainable Development Goals Series,
https://doi.org/10.1007/978-3-031-45663-3_8

have witnessed how money that could have been used to build good hospitals and promote healthcare programmes is misused by corrupt leaders.

Tracking Africa's stolen billions, an article on the United Nations Economic Commission of Africa website highlighted that the fight against African capital flight and illicit financial flows cost the continent between $50 billion and $148 billion annually. The amount looted and exported out of the continent is far above the amount it receives through financial aid yearly and far above the amount the World Bank said the continent needs annually to fast-track its infrastructural development. In September 2017, Peter Hain cried about a UK Bank linked to the Gupta family assisting the family in laundering money from South Africa. It was witnessed how FBME Bank's License was terminated in Tanzania for helping in money laundering. Nigerian leaders are involved in money laundering by carrying vast amounts of cash out of the country. Almost 30% of Africa's private wealth is outside Africa, while only 3% of South Asia's private wealth and 6% of East Asia are outside Asia. If Africa's private wealth is outside, how do we have enough capital for domestic investment? Similarly, many African leaders carry out money laundering through the smuggling of precious stones such as gold and diamonds sold in cash outside Africa because of their access to diplomatic passports.

Peter Tosh sang, "Everybody is talking about crime; tell me who the criminals are". Almost all African leaders speak against corruption; who are the criminals? Who is stealing Africa's resources and money? If African leaders preach against corruption and practise what they preach, Africa will be a haven! Mbalela's (2012) article published in South Africa Sowetan Newspaper on 6 July 2012 titled "Pikoli Lambasted Political Leaders" states that South Africa had developed into a "kleptocratic" state—losing R30-billion a year in social services corruption. Vusi Pikoli said, "Often we see political leaders steal public funds today but still occupy their office tomorrow. Then they are appointed to higher office the next day to do more damage to the economy". Pikoli throws light on the increase of corruption in South Africa by saying that the government is always claiming to be clamping down on corruption, yet they have not seen a rise according to Transparency International's corruption index. In 2010, South Africa ranked number 54 on the index, but in 2011, South Africa was at number 64. In October 2011, the head of the South Africa Special Investigation Unit (SIU), Willie Hofmeyr, told the National Assembly Portfolio Committee on Justice and Constitutional Development that corruption comprising government procurement costs South Africa almost 30 billion annually. Willie Hofmeyr said that this amount of money could escalate the annual budget of the Department of Basic Education by 20%, the Department of Health by 25%, or the entire criminal justice system by 30%. The amount could benefit South Africans by substantially building more schools, hospitals, and police stations and staffing them with better-paid doctors, teachers, and police officers. I used to think this kind of looting was only in West, Central, and Eastern Africa. It was a shock to know the high levels of corruption in South Africa, with grafts running into billions.

Hamann (2003) quoted George Bush's Speech on 28 May 2001 at the Second Global Forum on Fighting Corruption. The former president of the USA, George Bush, said, "The corruption of governmental institutions threatens the common aspirations of all honest members of the international community. It threatens our common interests in promoting political and economic stability, upholding core democratic values, ending the reign of dictators, and creating a level playing field for lawful business activities". White House (2009), Barak Obama, the former president of the USA, in Speaking to Parliament in Accra, Ghana, in July 2009 said "no country is going to generate wealth if its leaders exploit the economy to augment themselves or if police can be bought off by drug traffickers. Obama said that no business wants to invest in a place where the government skims 20 per cent off the top, or the leader of the Port Authority is corrupt. No person wants to live in a society where the rule of law gives way to the rule of brutality and bribery. That is not democracy; that is tyranny, even if occasionally you sprinkle an election in there, and now is the time for that style of governance to end". The World Bank Article Corruption Hunters Rally for Action against Fraud sees corruption as "among the greatest obstacles to economic and social development". Annan (2003), the former president of the United Nations, in his Statement On The Adoption By The General Assembly Of The United Nations Convention Against Corruption on 31 October 2003, made it clear that "Corruption hurts the poor disproportionately by diverting funds intended for development, undermining a government's ability to provide basic services, feeding inequality and injustice, and discouraging foreign investment and aid in adoption to United Nations Convention against Corruption by the General Assembly". He further states that corruption is a significant drain on the effective use of resources for education. Despite these forms of public awareness of the impact of corruption, the continent's leadership needs to be more accurate in its consequences.

Corruption has become acceptable in conducting business in many quarters of Africa. An example is the informal 10% kickbacks to leaders for awarding tenders and contracts. It will be essential to look at the corruption perception from 2012 to 2018, as summarised in Table 8.1 and Figs. 8.1, 8.2, and 8.3.

Note: According to Transparency International, a country's score indicates the perceptive level of public sector corruption on a scale of 0–100, where 0 means that a country is perceived as highly corrupt and 100 is perceived as very clean.

According to the table above, only five countries scored above 50 according to the index from 2012 to 2015. These countries are less corrupt than other African countries—Botswana, Cape Verde, Mauritius, Rwanda, and Seychelles. There are signs of improvement in reducing corruption in countries like Ghana, Senegal, Tunisia, and Liberia. Countries such as Ghana, Lesotho, Namibia, and São Tomé and Príncipe recorded a corruption index of 40 to 49, which is a good sign, but they need to put more effort into fighting corruption as good examples to other African countries. Only 9.3% of Africa's countries are less corrupt, scoring 50 to 64.

Africa Corruption Report for 2018, 2017, and 2016 are shown below to highlight a bleak picture of corruption in the continent for a decade.

The Transparency International website on 01/02/2019 stated, "This year's Corruption Perceptions Index (CPI) presents a largely gloomy picture for Africa—only eight of 49 countries score more than 43 out of 100 on the index. Despite commitments from African leaders to declare 2018 as the African Year of Anti-Corruption, this has yet to translate into concrete progress. Seychelles scores 66 out of 100, to put it at the top of the region. Botswana and Cape Verde follow Seychelles, with scores of 61 and 57, respectively. At the very bottom of the index for the seventh year in a row, Somalia scores 10 points, followed by South Sudan (13) to round out the lowest scores in the region. With an average score of just 32, sub-Saharan Africa is the lowest-scoring region on the index, followed closely by Eastern Europe and Central Asia, with an average score of 35". Countries that declined into corruption in 2018 are Ghana, Burundi, Congo, Mozambique, and Liberia. For a decade, Africa has had the worst average score of 35 compared to other continents. Cases of corruption were highlighted, such as Africa's biggest corruption scandal in Mozambique, where former finance minister and Credit Suisse banker Manuel Chang was charged with concealing more than US$2 billion of hidden loans and bribes. In February 2009, a French court held that

Table 8.1 Africa corruption index report 2012 to 2015

Country	*2012*		*2013*		*2014*		*2015*	
	Score	*Ranking*	*Score*	*Ranking*	*Score*	*Ranking*	*Score*	*Ranking*
Algeria	34	105	36	94	36	100	36	88
Angola	22	157	23	153	19	161	15	163
Benin	36	94	36	94	39	80	37	83
Botswana	64	30	64	30	63	31	63	28
Burkina Faso	38	83	38	83	38	85	38	76
Burundi	19	165	21	157	20	159	21	150
Cameroon	26	144	25	144	27	136	27	130
Cape Verde	60	39	58	41	57	42	55	40
Central Afr. Rep.	26	144	25	144	24	150	24	145
Chad	19	165	19	163	22	154	22	147
Comoros	28	133	28	127	26	142	26	138
Congo	26	144	22	154	23	152	23	146
DRC	21	160	22	154	22	154	22	147
Ivory Coast	29	130	27	136	32	115	32	107
Djibouti	36	94	36	94	34	107	–	–
Egypt	36	118	32	114	37	94	36	88
Equatorial Guinea	20	163	19	163	–	–	–	–
Eritrea	25	150	20	160	18	166	18	154
Ethiopia	33	113	33	111	33	110	33	103
Gabon	35	102	34	106	37	94	34	99
Gambia	34	105	28	127	29	126	28	123
Ghana	45	64	46	63	48	61	47	56
Guinea	24	154	24	150	25	145	25	139
Guinea-Bissau	25	150	19	163	19	161	17	158
Kenya	27	139	27	136	25	145	25	139
Lesotho	45	64	49	55	49	55	44	61
Liberia	41	75	38	83	37	94	37	83
Libya	21	160	15	172	18	166	16	161
Madagascar	32	118	28	127	28	133	28	123
Malawi	37	88	37	91	33	110	31	112
Mali	34	105	28	127	32	115	35	95
Mauritania	31	123	30	119	30	124	31	112
Mauritius	57	43	52	52	54	47	53	45
Morocco	37	88	37	91	39	80	36	88
Mozambique	31	123	30	119	31	119	31	112
Namibia	48	58	48	57	49	55	53	45
Niger	33	113	34	106	35	103	34	99
Nigeria	27	139	25	144	27	136	26	136
Rwanda	53	50	53	49	49	55	54	44

(*continued*)

Table 8.1 (continued)

Country	*2012*		*2013*		*2014*		*2015*	
	Score	*Ranking*	*Score*	*Ranking*	*Score*	*Ranking*	*Score*	*Ranking*
São Tomé and Príncipe	*42*	*72*	*42*	*72*	*42*	*76*	*42*	*66*
Senegal	*36*	*94*	*41*	*77*	*43*	*69*	*44*	*61*
Seychelles	*52*	*51*	*54*	*47*	*55*	*43*	*55*	*40*
Sierra Leone	*31*	*123*	*30*	*119*	*31*	*119*	*29*	*119*
Somalia	*8*	*174*	*8*	*175*	*8*	*174*	*8*	*167*
South Africa	*43*	*69*	*42*	*72*	*44*	*67*	*44*	*61*
Sudan	*13*	*173*	*11*	*174*	*11*	*173*	*12*	*165*
South Sudan	–	–	*14*	*173*	*15*	*171*	*15*	*163*
Swaziland	*37*	*88*	*39*	*82*	*43*	*69*	–	–
Tanzania	*35*	*102*	*33*	*111*	*31*	*119*	*30*	*117*
Togo	*30*	*128*	*29*	*123*	*29*	*126*	*32*	*107*
Tunisia	*41*	*75*	*41*	*77*	*40*	*79*	*38*	*76*
Uganda	*29*	*130*	*26*	*140*	*26*	*142*	*25*	*139*
Zambia	37	88	38	83	38	85	38	76
Zimbabwe	20	163	21	157	21	156	21	150

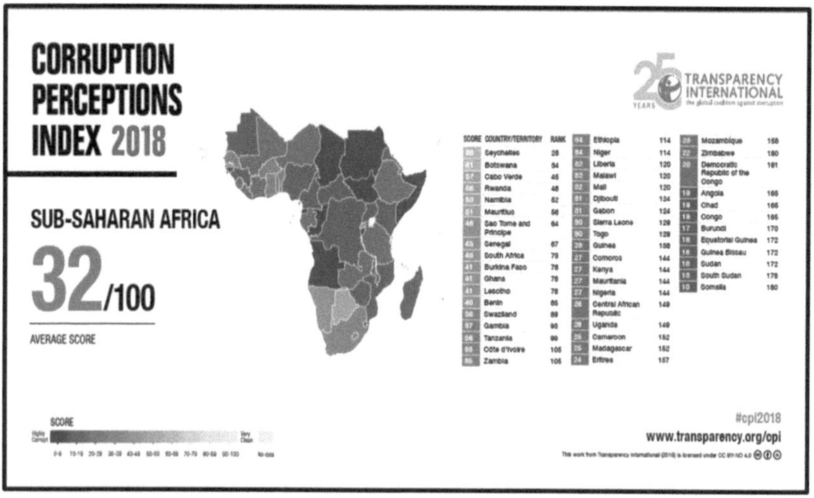

Fig. 8.1 Sub-Saharan Africa corruption index 2018

Fig. 8.2 Sub-Saharan Africa corruption index 2017

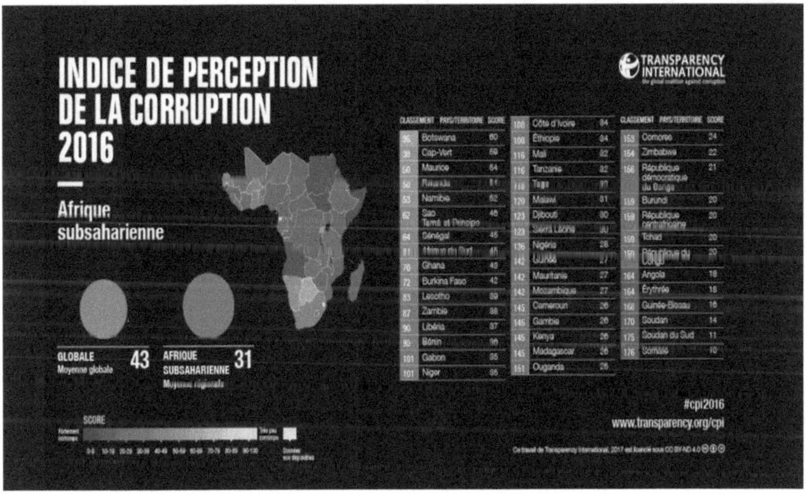

Fig. 8.3 Sub-Saharan Africa corruption index 2016

Omar Bongo's nine bank accounts were frozen with several millions of euros. The former president's son, Jose Filomeno dos Santos, was charged with making a fraudulent US$500 million transaction from Angola's sovereign wealth fund.

Africa's big brothers, including South Africa and Nigeria, have their share of corruption and the image of fighting it. While South Africa initiated a commission of inquiry into corruption headed by Zondo, where many revelations have been made, Nigeria, where the president was elected on the platform to fight corruption, has failed. Instead, the Muhammadu Buhari government used corruption as intimidation against the opposition, which was unsuccessful. Numerous corruption cases that reared their ugly head in his government were overlooked.

Igwe (2012a) wrote an article, "President Obiang and kleptocrats in Africa", published on Pambazuka news on 14 March 2012, reported, "On 29 September, 2011, in faraway Paris, the French Police swooped on a compound allegedly belonging to one of the longest serving dictators in Africa, President of Equatorial Guinea and current Chairman of African Union, Teodoro Obiang Nguema Mbasogo, and seized eleven luxury cars. Amongst the cars seized were two Buggatti Veyrons, three Ferraris, one Porsche Carrera GT and Bentleys with a total value of $5m". Uche Igwe further states that a former Nigeria Attorney General and Minister for Justice of Nigeria, Mohammed Bello Adoke, said that about $20 billion to $40 billions of global inflow of proceeds of corruption and criminality originate from monies handed as bribes to public officials in developing countries.

On 10 February 2020, a French court ruled against Teodorin Obiang, the vice president of Equatorial Guinea, in a years-long embezzlement. Teodorin Obiang was ordered to pay a fine of €30 million (R490 196,078; $32.9 million). He was given a three-year suspended jail term after a lower court found him guilty of graft and money laundering charges. During these years of court cases, a Paris appeals court confirmed the seizure of his property, including a six-level mansion in Paris, which had been valued at €107 million in 2012. The looted money could be used to build infrastructure and social facilities to sustainably develop the country.

Similarly, corruption in the education system is worsening and pervasive. According to VOA news, "With tens of millions of dollars already missing in Kenya's Ministry of Education, the corruption scandal currently rocking Kenya's schools threatens to cost the country millions more. In the parliament, finance Minister Uhuru Kenyatta presented the results of an internal investigation which found that over 4.2 billion Kenyan shillings—about $46 million—was missing from the ministry of Education. More specifically, Kenyatta revealed the money had been stolen from President Mwai Kibaki's landmark initiative to provide free primary education for every Kenyan" http://m.voanews.com/158335.html.

Bold et al. (2017) noted that teacher absenteeism is widespread in Africa, indicating that overall absenteeism in classes in Africa is 44%. Nigeria records the lowest with 23%, while the highest is Uganda at 57%. School attendance stands at 23%, the lowest in Kenya, record at 15%, and the highest is Mozambique at 45%. In Nigeria and many other African countries, teacher absenteeism is a typical tragedy; many teachers would rather do their private jobs or private teaching than be in public schools where they are employed and earn salaries. Teachers' absenteeism worsens in Nigeria because of government delays in paying salaries. In Nigeria, some state governments owe teachers more than four to eight months of wages. Transparency International reported that in 2010, 64% of schools surveyed in Africa published no accounting information; 64% of schools are run without leadership accountability and good governance. How does the continent progress without proper accountability in an institution that produces leaders and workers?

Corruption in education has affected almost every aspect of the system, such as the leaking of examination papers that impacts the quality of results, consequently influencing sustainable economic growth. When students learn how to give bribes in schools, buy leaked examination papers, and "see" teachers or lecturers for marks or to gain admission, and when many teachers are always absent from classes without reason, the education systems teach them that corruption is normal. These impact the continent's development as it preys on the fabrics required for sustainable development.

Justice Initiative's (2010) report on Equatorial Guinea indicated that teachers with political connections but no experience or accreditation were hired, even though they rarely appeared at the classes they purportedly taught. Qualified people cannot get jobs, and those who are not eligible get jobs because of political connections. Nepotism and favouritism are rampant in all the government sectors in the continent, endangering sustainable development. Bennett (2001) states that just because the teacher is present does not mean that any teaching takes place often; he has visited schools in Ethiopia, Ghana, Cameroon, and Nepal and found the school open, but both the teacher and his students are absent. He also states that he witnessed where a teacher has taken the children to work on his farm, not as a learning experience as might be obtained from a demonstration plot, but as unpaid child labour for the teacher's benefit.

In the colonial period, Western banks were complaisant to the corrupt activities in Africa, and presently, some Western banks, to an extent, are aiding the corrupt activities of the post-colonial leaders and political elites. Mbeki (2009, p. 25) observed that "Even the mighty Western oil companies have not escaped the destructive power of Africa's political elites and are periodically compelled to make huge payments into the foreign private bank accounts of the heads of states—and their families and friends—of oil-producing countries. For instance, the United States Senate has uncovered vast sums paid by oil companies into the private bank accounts in Washington, DC, of Equatorial Guinea's head of state". The appointment of directors in most government financial institutions in Africa contributes to financial corruption. Most positions are based on patronage and tribal and political affiliations rather than qualification, ethics, and professionalism. When the management of financial institutions is in the hands of people who are not ethical and do not know what it takes to manage a financial institution, it affects the profitability and sustainability of the financial institution and the development of society. These unqualified people are appointed to give out fraudulent loans or directions for illegal activities that affect the economic and social development of the continent.

Fighting corruption has been a global community concern. Many private and public institutions have joined forces in fighting corruption because it hurts sustainable development, undermines good governance, and threatens democracy. In Africa, fighting corruption has been in many forms, mainly through establishing organisations whose only goal is fighting corruption. However, some of these organisations have been misguided that their efforts to fight corruption and minimise its impact are impractical. On the surface, many of these organisations cut the image of anti-corruption, while behind the scenes, they are corrupt institutions with political agendas. Corruption within the anti-corruption institutions is rampant because of political interference and a tool against perceived political enemies. This is why new governments and presidents always find it easy to remove leaders of anti-corruption organisations for their own selfish interests. Where the leaders of anti-corruption organisations were not fired, sometimes the organisations were disbanded to change the structure to protect incoming presidents or fight a dirty political war for the coming governments. For instance, many anti-corruption organisations have been dissolved in Nigeria due to leadership searching for loyalty rather than fighting corruption. An excellent example in Nigeria is Operation Purge the Nation in 1975, War against Discipline in 1983, and Economic and Financial Crime Commission in 2004. In South Africa, we witnessed the disbandment of Scorpion by the government due to their fierce independence needed for anti-corruption fights and established HAWKS.

The campaign against corruption has an ugly strategy in Africa. It has become a campaign against political rivals, suppression of some political parties, and silencing minority parties and ethnic groups in a political setting rather than an instrument to flush out corruption. This is one reason there is little result in wars against corruption in Africa. Some countries are fighting corruption through sound policies, strategies, and innovative IT systems, which have yielded some results. However, these successes are tiny compared to the corruption level in many countries. Being a leader of an anti-corruption organisation in Africa is difficult because of political interference. It is like being trapped between the devil and the deep blue sea. However, anti-corruption organisation leaders should be loyal to their countries. Still, in most cases, they have been dedicated to the executives that appointed them or to the political party in power against the national interest and a real fight against corruption.

Anti-corruption agencies have varying strengths in capacity and resources and often need more resources to carry out their functions effectively. Strengthening anti-corruption organisations has not been the priority of the leaders and political elites because they are the architects of corruption. To alleviate corruption, anti-corruption organisations should be strengthened and capacitated. The head of the anti-corruption organisations should be appointed by civil society bodies, legislators, and the private sector. When a president has to select a leader of the anti-corruption organisation, it must be approved by civil society, legislators, and private sector organisations. Observing such a principle in Africa will be hard for leadership because of the selfish agenda. Corruption in Africa is killing businesses, harmful to economic growth, and devastating to economic growth, the citizens, the livelihood systems, and the values and morals of a society. A corrupt leader is a household destroyer, a creator of poverty, anti-economic and social development, and an architect of underdevelopment.

CHAPTER 9

African Conflict

9.1 Conflicts

For almost five decades, between the 1960s and 2015, there have been more than 75 violent changes of governments in sub-Saharan Africa. It is sad that between 2000 and 2018, up to 18 African countries have witnessed armed rebellion, and many more have experienced political crises. "Africa is worse afflicted than any other continent; in 1999, one in five Africans lived in a country racked by civil or cross-border war. Ninety per cent of the casualties were civilians. Nineteen million Africans were forced to flee their homes. And an estimated 20 million landmarks lurked beneath African soil" (Guest 2004, p. 54).

Many African conflicts are self-inflicted and ethnicity-motivated due to natural resources, religious beliefs, economic rents, illegal mining, and political ambitions clashes. When people thought Africa was about to have a breathing space and reduce the number of ongoing conflicts, new conflicts resurfaced and gained momentum, with many civilian deaths in South Sudan, Sudan, Nigeria, Central African Republic, Burundi, DRC, and Mozambique.

Greed is creating a new kind of conflict in mining areas and is common in mining areas of Africa where there is gold, diamond, and oil. In the Niger Delta area of Nigeria, politicians were pointing fingers at each other in the early 2000s for supporting illegal oil mining while kidnapping and

C. E. Osuigwe, *Leadership and Economic Development Challenges in Post-Colonial Africa*, Sustainable Development Goals Series,
https://doi.org/10.1007/978-3-031-45663-3_9

blowing of oil pipelines were norms. The illegal mining of gold in Zamfara in Nigeria has led to the killing of thousands of people. Mining diamonds and gold is fuelling conflicts and crises in Zimbabwe and DR Congo. In Marikana, in South Africa, 32 miners were shot by police because of a lack of leadership negotiation strategy and recklessness. Apart from significant conflicts making news, there are always minor conflicts rearing their ugly heads in all the corners of Africa over agricultural land. Numerous community clashes over grazing land and using natural water (rivers, streams, and springs), particularly in Nigeria, West Africa, and part of East Africa, between herdsmen and farmers, led to thousands of deaths.

The impacts of conflicts are enormous, from the killing of defenceless women and children to an increase in poverty, to high unemployment, to the destruction of infrastructure, environment, tourism potentials, the livelihood of the poor, and thwarting all efforts for regional integration, to financial leakages, and so many others. All these affect the well-being of Africans. According to Oxfam International (2007) report titled "Africa's Missing Billions", Africa has squandered more than $284 billion on conflicts and wars and suffered immensely from conflict and armed violence. Oxfam report further highlighted that human disasters and armed conflict cost Africa around $18 billion annually. This was a financial waste, utterly devastating to Africa's development. The financial report by Oxfam does not include wasted human resources, which, if measured accurately, could be in billions of dollars. The report cited global arms trade as a primary contributor to the violence that had claimed millions of African lives and affected Africa's economic growth. The Oxfam report stressed that the costs of war could solve the Human Immune Deficiency Virus and the Acquired Immune Deficiency Syndrome (HIV/AIDS) pandemic, prevent tuberculosis and malaria, and provide clean water, sanitation, and education. According to the report, the continent lost 15% of its GDP, representing an enormous economic burden. The 15% also represents one and a half times the average African spending on health and education combined.

Conflict is devastating to infrastructure and investment. Also, it leads to the migration of skills needed for the development of Africa. Many professionals have left Africa for Europe, Canada, Asia, and the USA because of conflicts. These affect economic development and growth. Similarly, trading links must be more active, hindering regional development and integration. Furthermore, conflicts encourage illegal mining, hijack the market system, and devastate the economy by robbing it of taxes that could be used for development.

The selfish interests of predatory political elites are the main reasons the continent's conflicts still need to be resolved. The voracious interest fuels inter-country conflicts by predatory elites capitalising on ethnic emotions to instigate conflicts. During Uganda's conflict, for example, Tanzania supported Yoweri Museveni as a rebel leader of the National Redemption Front (NRF). Many rebel groups who fought to seize power in DR Congo had the blessing of Uganda's and Rwanda's political elites and leaders, as highlighted by the UN (2001) report titled "Security Council Condemns Illegal Exploitation of Democratic Republic of Congo's Natural Resources". The cross-border conflict between Eritrea and Ethiopia has its own ethnic emotional challenges. During the conflicts in Liberia and Sierra Leone, there were accusations of Burkina Faso's leadership involvement. These interregional conflicts affect the integration of Africa and regions economically and socially. The herdsmen conflicts and crisis are a West African crisscross boundary. The Boko Haram (Western education is forbidden) conflict in Nigeria has its own cross-border ethnic network. Boko Haram affect economic and infrastructural development integration within the broader region of Northeastern Nigeria, Northwestern Cameroon, and Southern Chad. This region has witnessed high levels of underdevelopment due to this conflict.

Conflicts in Africa have devastating consequences for landlocked countries. Due to the conflicts in Angola and Mozambique, some countries, such as Malawi and Zimbabwe, needed help exporting and importing goods. Specifically, the conflict in Mozambique led to high export and import costs for Malawi businesses. It slowed economic growth in Malawi during the period, although Malawi's financial problems could not be linked to Mozambique's conflicts alone.

Conflicts sever rural agricultural production through damages to agriculture infrastructures, farms, and small-scale irrigation facilities. Conflicts disrupt market networks and accessibility between urban and rural areas, endangering the survival of rural farmers and businesses. In 2022, the Nigeria Bureau of Statistics stated that Northeast Nigeria has the highest population living under multidimensional poverty. This is possible because of the devastating effect of the Boko Haram Conflict in the Northeast of Nigeria.

Conflicts in the continent have a shattering effect on schooling and education. It increases school dropouts and poor enrolment rates in primary, secondary, high schools, and universities. Education for All Global Monitoring Report (2011) states that 42% of out-of-school children live in conflict-affected countries. It signposted the incidence of attacks on schools and violence against children and teachers. It further emphasises the impact of lost education opportunities and the reinforcement of poverty, unemployment, and marginalisation that drive further conflicts. In Mozambique, the civil war from 1977 to 1992 caused the loss of 5.3 years of schooling. Even short episodes of violence can be associated with significant setbacks. In Northeastern Nigeria, conflicts led to the loss of education periods of more than two years for some schools. In Rwanda, an interruption in education in the early 1990s translated into a loss of 1.2 years of schooling. Conflicts not only cause loss of schooling years; they also destroy educational infrastructure and facilities. In Sierra Leone, educational infrastructure was damaged in the country's civil war. Many schools required rehabilitation. In 2009, many schools were closed in Mogadishu due to conflicts, while some were occupied by armed forces. Conflict is dangerous to school children and children of schooling age; enlisting children as soldiers who were supposed to be schooling is common in Africa. Fear and insecurity associated with sexual violence keep young girls off school.

Global Coalition (2004) states that about 800,000 Rwandans were reportedly massacred; the Burundi civil war claimed over 200,000 lives as of the year 2000; in Liberia, over 250,000 lives were lost in the country's 14-year civil war between 1990 and 2004; in Sierra Leone, it is estimated to be around 200,000 people who were killed between 1991 and 2001. The most pathetic situation occurred in Sudan. The civil war in Sudan has been one of the longest in the continent, with an estimated two million lives lost to the war and 4.7 million displaced (Global Coalition 2004, p. 10). Around 30 million internally displaced persons, refugees, and asylum seekers live in Africa, representing almost one-third of the world's refugee population. Millions of new displacements were recorded in the Democratic Republic of the Congo, Ethiopia, Central African Republic, South Sudan, and Nigeria, triggered by increasing insecurity and human rights violations (UNHCR ----). UNHRC further reported that millions of people have fled their homes in the East and Horn of Africa and the Great Lakes region due to conflict, climate-related events, and political violence. By the end of 2021, the region hosted 4.9 million refugees, asylum seekers, and 12 million internally displaced people. South Africa seems to be at war with itself; police statistics in 2021 show that the number of people murdered was about 20,000. In three months of April to June 2022 in South Africa, about 6424 were killed through gun violence.

Africa has found it problematic to emerge from conflicts to excellent and transparent government because of conflict rooted in ethnic hatred, bigotry, religious practices, and devastation of community livelihood. Countries in many parts of the world, including Europe, Asia, and America, have emerged from conflicts into better states. Some people believe that governments and society need conflicts before they can know the need for true reform for political, social, and economic development. In Africa, it is a different situation; conflicts have ways of recycling. They act like a chameleon, changing their modus operandi per predatory political elites' selfish agenda.

Many conflicts have sprouted up because of ethnopolitical party alliances and religious differences. Such conflicts have destroyed properties, infrastructure and goods and services in Niger, Nigeria, Mali, Chad, Uganda, and Kenya. In Kenya, an ethnic conflict that pitted the Kikuyu against the Luos and Kalenjin and resulted in 1500 deaths was because of the result of the 2007 election. The civil war in Sudan lasted over four decades between the Arab Muslim North and Non-Arab Christian South. The Rwanda genocide that resulted in the killing of more than 700 thousand Tutsis and moderate Hutus is ethnic evil. The tension between Tutsis and Hutus in Burundi is always manifesting, and the pressure and conflicts have cost more than 100,000 lives since 1972. The Nigeria/Biafra war of 1966 to 1970 has its own ethnic connotation and elements of religion and claimed more than 3 million lives. There have been ongoing ethnic conflicts between the Fulani nomadic herdsmen and the indigenous tribes of Plateau State and Benue State in Nigeria over agricultural land for animal grazing and crop production. The Boko Haram conflict in Nigeria is deeply rooted in religion but hijacked by a few political elites who use it as a political instrument.

Conflicts in Africa are the major contributors to the refugee crisis in Africa and pose a significant problem to the social and economic development of the continent. According to the United Nations Refugee Agency, around 30 million internally displaced persons, refugees, and asylum seekers live in Africa, representing almost one-third of the world's refugee population. The challenges African refugees face are numerous, which include xenophobic attacks, torture, killing, harassment, and extortion by law enforcement agents. From 1990 to 2015, about 18,500 people were known to have died on dangerous trips from North Africa to Italy, Spain, and Malta; they were African refugees running away from conflicts and economic hardships. The death toll is probably higher than the figures mentioned. Despite the awareness of the rise of deaths of refugees trying to cross over from North Africa to Europe, refugees are not deterred from embarking on this dangerous journey. These refugees originally come from sub-Saharan Africa and would have made the long overland trips to North Africa by foot or by bus to find work. In Libya and South Africa, xenophobia is expressed in accusations of criminality, verbal and physical attacks, harassment, arbitrary detention, and torture. In 2005, about 20 migrants were killed in Egypt when the police confronted Sudanese refugees and migrants demonstrating in a camp in Cairo.

On a Special Assignment on 22 May 2007, a Methodist pastor based in Johannesburg described the refugees' influx to South Africa as a blessing. Do South Africans see it as a blessing? It is crucial to exploit opportunities that come with refugees as far as it adds value to development. The influx of a refugee in a country could reduce per capita income, but in the long run, it will increase each person's capital income as refugees create jobs directly or indirectly. Refugees are redundant labour and could be captured into the developmental strategy that will yield financial benefits in any African country. Refugees boost human and capital resources, which should be addressed. Refugees can challenge a growing economy if not properly managed and utilised. Channelling refugee skills can contribute immensely to economic development as refugees come with skills. In many parts of Africa, refugee businesses are growing. Many come with technical knowledge in auto repair, building, teaching, construction, electrical, small-scale companies, furniture making, fashion design, and other technical skills. Most of these refugees are entrepreneurial and employ locals where they reside, particularly in Africa. Africa has a problem: poor leadership that cannot find the best ways to utilise refugees' social and economic development skills. In the West, refugees' skills and knowledge are harnessed for industrial and economic production. Many African countries need proper leaders, which will come with little cost but with vision and understanding of what the continent needs for its development.

Building peace in Africa has not yielded much result because of ethnic biases and incomprehensive consultations. Communities have been sidelined in peace negotiations in many African countries during conflict resolutions and peace negotiations, and the processes do not allow affected communities or people to be a part of conflict resolutions. Averting conflicts involves identifying the root of the conflicts and strategising how to solve the problem, including the involvement of aggrieved citizens. If conflicts in Africa are minimal or have been minimised, the continent will have more sustainable development; some of the children killed could have become great people helping to develop the continent, taking care of families, and growing the economy.

If the consequences of conflicts are elaborated, more than 1000 pages of the book will be needed to cover it. The few mentioned above are for reference.

9.2 A Summary of a Short Story Depicting an Aspect of African Conflict Problems

Ilibagiza's (2006) book *Left to Tell* expresses her story.

Immaculée Ilibagiza narrated her story of surviving the Rwandan genocide in her book *Left to Tell.* She was born in paradise, which is how she felt about her homeland. In 1994, the peaceful society in which she grew up was ripped apart by Rwanda's bloody holocaust. Her family was brutally murdered during a killing spree that lasted for three months and claimed the lives of more than 800,000 Rwandans. Extraordinarily, she survived the human carnage driven by the then Rwandan's predatory political elites and leaders. In her story, she and seven other women huddled silently together in the cramped bathroom of a local pastor for 91 days while hundreds of machete-wielding killers hunted for them. She said, "I heard the killers call my name. They were on the other side of the wall, and less than an inch of plaster and wood separated us. Their voices were cold, hard, and determined. She is here … we know she's some where, find her—find Immaculee. There were many voices, many killers. I could see them in my mind: my former friends and neighbours, who had always greeted me with love and kindness, moving through the house carrying spears and machetes and calling names". "I have killed 399 cockroaches", said one of the killers. "Immaculee will make 400. It's a good number to kill".

This is a retrogressive heritage of ethnicity in Africa, under the watchful eye of its leaders, political elites, and the African Union. It is a sad story of senseless killing, driven by extreme crazy and ethnic illusion and propelled by leadership madness. When Africans are killing themselves, other continents are mobilising their ethnic and social differences for the development of their continent, particularly in Asia. In Africa, ethnicity is a blessing but mobilised by some political elites as a curse rather than a force for development.

CHAPTER 10

Women, Children, and Youths Issues

10.1 African Women

Women represent more than half of the African population of 1.2 billion. Abbas (2018) highlighted, "Women grow 70% of Africa's food but have few rights over the land they tend". The level of involvement of African women in economic growth without the security of economic rent or ownership is devastating to their protection of life. After the celebrated World Women Conference in Beijing in 1995, women all over the world expected a positive change in their lives. There was the development of policies and strategies for gender parity. There was the Convention on the Elimination of Discrimination against Women, but human rights abuses against women go unnoticed because of poor implementation. There are achievements made, but there is still more to be done for women's right to justice, economic and social.

In the pre-colonial period, women played a vital role in developing many African communities, empires, and kingdoms. Queen Amina of Zaria in present-day Northern Nigeria was a warrior and led men to war. There is the story of Queen Hangbe and her elite female warriors of the Dahomey Empire in the present-day Southern Benin Republic. The story of Queen Amanirenas, who ruled the kingdom of Kush in present-day Sudan. There was Queen Nzinga Mbanda, who led the Mbundu people; Queen Asantewaa, who protected the golden stool in Ghana; and many

C. E. Osuigwe, *Leadership and Economic Development Challenges in Post-Colonial Africa*, Sustainable Development Goals Series,
https://doi.org/10.1007/978-3-031-45663-3_10

others. There was also a widow of the Nguni king of Mozambique, who became a priest in charge of a shrine for her husband's burial. The power of kings' wives and queen-mothers was addressed in most African kingdoms and empires' political, economic, and social affairs. In pre-colonial Igbo society, the power of Umu Ada (Association of First Daughters) cannot be disregarded in the justice, economic, social, and policymaking of the Igbo communities. Their contribution through a united voice immensely impacted Nigeria's pre-colonial, colonial, and post-colonial periods. In various ways, African societies engaged women in development decisions and the distribution of resources.

Similarly, African women played a significant role in the continent's liberation. For example, the Aba women's riot of November 1929 in Nigeria fought against the British colonial government's imposition of taxation on women. The incident of the Aba women riot started at Oloko, a village in Bende Division in colonial Eastern Nigeria and spread to all parts of Igbo land. Nwanyereuwa, a village peasant woman, challenged the foundation of British authority in Nigeria by refusing to be registered for an impending colonial tax. The revolt in Oloko Bende quickly spread to many parts of the Owerri and Calabar provinces, turning into an all-out revolution against all aspects of the political institution and the European trading companies. Thousands of villages and ordinary women took matters into their own hands, stormed colonial administrative centres, and then later to the important commercial city of Aba, which housed several European trading companies. They took on the warrant chiefs the colonial government selected, demanding caps (the most important symbol of their authority). This single act by Igbo women demystified the colonial leadership and their control over the various communities and contributed to the fight for independence in Nigeria. The black women's emancipation in South Africa is fascinating. The march against using racial Identity Documents (ID) to travel to towns during the apartheid era was vital in dethroning the apartheid regime. Despite the above, post-colonial Africa has discarded the role of women in leadership in most parts of Africa.

The present challenge of African women is overwhelming. There are limited policies or limitations on approaches to enhance women's participation in development and to enable or bridge the gap of gender discrepancy. Going through many poverty reduction policies initiated by many African countries, they need to recognise the disparity between the income of men and women or access to opportunities within their communities. Lack of recognition of the differences does not make it possible to strategise the best way to empower women. The disparities are experienced in women's representation in governments and bodies that make laws and regulations.

Women's representation in the parliament could be better and more adequate in many countries. It influences the development of policies or laws that do not encourage gender equality for social and economic development. Nevertheless, some countries have good women representatives in the legislative arm of government. There are exceptional cases in Rwanda, Seychelles, South Africa, Senegal, and Mozambique. These countries were among the top 20 countries in the world in 2017 that promoted women's participation and representation. Rwanda has proven to be a country going in the right direction. Rwanda's corruption index has been above five for more than four years, and the country ranks number 1 in the world in women's involvement in politics and representation in parliament. Nigeria has more than 180 million people, with a female population percentage of 49.38%, almost equal to its male population. Nigerian women's representation in the Lower House stood at 6.8% and in the Upper House at 6.4% in 2011. The percentage of the female population and their participation in the law-making body is cause for concern. This shows how Nigerian political elites are unfriendly towards the participation of women in government.

There are limitations to policies and strategies to improve women's participation in decision-making. As a result, women are underrepresented in decision-making positions in governments, civil society, and the private sector in almost all African countries. Few women who have participated in the development of Africa have been outstanding. In 2014, Time Magazine named Ngozi Okonjo Iweala among the 100 influential people in the world. In 2015, Ngozi Okonjo Iweala and Ellen Johnson-Sirleaf were named by Forbes among the 50 most influential people in the world. Wangari Maathai won the Nobel Peace Prize in 2004. Before that, she won the Right Livelihood Award in 1986. Nkosazana Dlamini-Zuma led the African Union in the right direction, helped transform the organisation and instilled professionalism in executing work. The role of Ellen Johnson Sirleaf, the former president of Liberia, in steering the war-torn economy of Liberia to good standing was outstanding. Where women were ministers in any country in Africa, they were exceptional when compared to many of their male counterparts. It is not a blanket situation because there were corrupt women, but the percentage was minimal.

The challenges African women face daily are gender inequality, income disparity, social and economic status of women, gender-based violence and access to infrastructure, particularly water and sanitation and job position. Similarly, in rural areas, women walk up to five kilometres on average to fetch water for domestic use and drinking daily. It reduces the time and energy needed to empower themselves. It also affects the performance of schoolgirls, as the tasks of fetching water and firewood are carried out mainly by women and girls.

The crisis that limits women's potential in the labour market begins with the challenge of a girl child's education. Even educated women often find themselves employed in low-paying jobs, unlike their male counterparts. Only a good policy can address this challenge. For example, South Africa has employment equity that gives women preference for employment opportunities. In some countries like Ghana and Nigeria, women's participation in the labour market is also high but in very low-paid jobs, particularly in the informal economy. A short story by Eucharia Mbachu, and I captured this story in this book to express the impact of leadership on girls' child migration to Europe and its consequences.

The short story is highlighted below from a social media post of Eucharia Mbachu. "As a young girl in, I witnessed firsthand, how these girls were being maltreated worse than slaves. Some of them had no place to sleep unless their pimps take them home. On many occasions, I brought several to my apartment and sacrifice my own money to help them return home. At a point, I organised some friends and we pressured the Nigerian Embassy in Rome to do something to help the girls. But nothing was done. In one case that shocked the very fabric of my life was when I met a 12-year-old child without sweater and with an open sandal shoe, shivering on the street on a cold winter. I took her home, nursed her for about two weeks and then took her to the Nigerian Embassy. I wanted the Ambassador and his wife to take her in until her ticket money could be arranged. But they came up with these long protocols that made no sense to me".

"As nothing happened, we went back to my apartment. I told the story to one of my professors, who helped take her case to the authorities. The Questura in Rome gave her a choice to stay with a document and go to school or be bought a ticket to go home. Already traumatised, she said she would prefer to return to her mother".

This story ended well, but many of these young girls experienced daily trauma and hardship with no one to save their situation. Some parents had to sell their lands to send their daughters overseas to work or study, but many worked as sex slaves. Child marriage in many parts of Africa is another irresponsible act that disempowers a girl child. In the face of the challenges that make the economy bleed, African leaders seem to be in a comfort zone.

10.2 African Children

Children are the hope of the future. The importance of children to a country's economy is measured by the premium placed on their health. A good child healthcare foundation must be laid to have a healthy population. The challenges of children in Africa are summarised below:

1. Women and girls from sub-Saharan Africa are also trafficked into modern slavery in Europe, particularly domestic servitude and commercial sexual exploitation. Nigeria is a source for persons trafficked to Europe, particularly women exploited in Italy, Belgium, France, Spain, Sweden, and the Netherlands. Sub-Saharan Africa has the largest share of child trafficking in the world (Anti-Slavery Commissioner 2016)
2. It is estimated that approximately 120,000 children between the ages of 7 and 18 have participated in armed conflicts throughout the African continent (ILO 2003)
3. The number of stunted children has fallen in all regions except sub-Saharan Africa, which increased by about one-third between 1990 and 2013
4. In sub-Saharan Africa, measles takes a child's life nearly every minute of every day. The effective measles vaccine costs as little as $1 per child. (Source: UNICEF)
5. Sub-Saharan Africa is the only region where the number of people without access to water is growing. In the last 20 years, 37 million more Africans have been without water and 247 million more with out sanitation. 180,000 children under the age of five die each year in sub-Saharan Africa from diarrheal diseases caused by a lack of water, sanitation, and hygiene services. In addition, rural areas are disproportionately affected; 85% of those without water and 70% without sanitation live in rural areas. Clean and accessible water is critical to human health and a healthy environment. It is also an essential pillar of development, published on the World Bank Website (Gouredou 2023)

6. 418 million population in Africa lacks even a basic level of drinking water service, 779 million lack essential sanitation services (including 208 million who still practise open defecation), and 839 million still lack essential hygiene services.
7. Of 57 million global out-of-school children of primary school age in 2015, 33 million are in sub-Saharan Africa, and more than half (55%) are girls. An estimated 50% of out-of-school children will never go to school.

The report above highlights some of the predicaments African children are going through. Many of these cases could have been prevented or minimised if political elites and leaders were serious about serving and saving the continent's future. Every minute of the day, one child dies of measles, yet a measles vaccine is less than $1, while billions are looted from government treasurers across Africa daily. Due to leaders' lack of attention, children's health, education, and social welfare are severely hampered by social and economic conditions.

Children, women, and the youth are the primary victims of all the major African conflicts. In war-torn areas of Africa and conflict zones, children are forcibly recruited by rebels and used as child soldiers or killed. They face exploitation, rape, and torture if they attempt to escape. Guest R. (2004, p. 52) said, "What scared me most about Congo was not the shouting, stone-throwing crowds, nor the rattle of gunfire, nor the occasional dead body dumped by the side of the road. It was the sight of a boy soldier—he looked no more than twelve, but he might have been a malnourished fifteen—sitting on a step, resting his chin on the barrel of his AK-47". The pain is that the child soldiers are destroyed psychologically and abandoned after the selfish ambitions of the political elite have been achieved. Rebels and guerrilla movements that use child soldiers are killing the fabric that holds Africans together. Recruiting children as soldiers is preying on economic growth and on the future existence of the continent.

Children who escaped the disaster of conflicts have faced problems such as lack of shelter, food shortage, and inadequate facilities and infrastructures. Children who lost their parents become heads of the household, leading to a vicious cycle of poverty. Once in this situation, they become a political elites' target that leverages them to instigate violence and conflicts.

In conflict areas, young girls forcefully or unwillingly offer themselves to rebels or government soldiers to protect their families or siblings. One of the atrocities of rebels in Africa was subjection to anti-social acts, such as girls being forced to sleep with their fathers and their mothers sleeping with their sons. They sexually assault young girls and take them as domestic slaves or sex slaves. These wicked acts impact the spirit of their survival. Most of these atrocities go unchecked, unpunished.

10.3 The Predicament of African Youth

Africa has the youngest youth population in the world and is experiencing a youth bulge. According to the African Union, the continent has almost 420 million youths, and one-third are unemployed. Most of the youth are vulnerably employed and need to figure out their permanent job status. In the South Africa Human Science and Research Council (HSRC) presentation, Professor Monde Makiwane and Mr. Chukwuemeka Osuigwe portrayed the existing youth bulge in Africa and its expected consequences, if not urgently tackled. Professor Makiwane highlighted the increase in the youth population in Africa that results in youth bulge and its effects on the rise in unemployment in Africa. Makiwane and Osuigwe interrogated whether the youth bulge in sub-Saharan Africa would be like the Asian Miracle that encouraged and assisted the economic growth of many Asian countries or the North African Arab uprising? Why is it a challenge in Africa instead of a blessing? It is rooted in bad and weak leadership that needs a comprehensive vision for youth development. Where there are good policies and strategies for youth development, corruption and conflicts derail their implementations to enhance youth empowerment and entrepreneurship.

The youths' aspiration faces challenges of marginalisation, disregard for policy development, and gerontocratic social and political order. Youth expressing their concerns could be regarded as disrespectful in many African countries. Often, the youth have been condemned to the periphery of decision-making. On many occasions, the old political brigades in Africa shy away from healthy debates or conversations with the youth that will enhance sustainable development. It is about a healthy political dialogue to strengthen good governance and hold leaders accountable.

The limitation of youthful voices is the peripheral position they have found themselves in and the need for mentoring. Lack of mentorship has devastating effects on the transition of power and responsibility. It has also been shown through business failures where teams of business leaders were successful, and their immediate successors failed. Tito Mboweni, former Governor of the South African Reserve Bank, said, "For those of us schooled in the old ANC traditions, some of the behaviours might have been a bit unbecoming. But we must live with what we have sown. We have not educated the youth sufficiently about the traditions of the party as we have taken advantage of their energy to use them as voting fodders". Mboweni is correct, although he was being diplomatic about it. The old brigades still think they should have a monopoly of power and governance. It results in manifestations of elongation of terms in many countries. It highlights the subservient political environment in which political leaders operate. Mboweni said we reap what we sow, indicating that the continent's development challenges are intertwined with poor youth participation and a lack of good mentoring of the youth by leadership. It exposes the old politicians' need for more confidence in the youth, which is hard to bear in a continent where the youth are energetic and promising. The youth desperately seek a voice in Africa, where basic leadership structures are not favourable to listening to their voices; examples were the university protests in South Africa and the EndSars protest in Nigeria. Still, there is a growing trend that today's youth no longer accept or respect those structures and increasingly demand a voice of their own. This has challenged the status quo that has bedevilled Africa's development.

Youth prospects should be integrated into the mainstream of the economy. There is neither hope of choosing a type of work that suits their dream goals nor starting a business that serves the ideas they are harbouring. The youth can establish productive and creative industries by harnessing the right combination of motivation, ideas, and opportunities. This will lead to the youth transiting from being "job seekers" to "job creators" and moving from social and economic dependency to self-sufficiency, thereby contributing to society and the upkeep of their families, and leading roles in the communities and the countries.

The youth bulge is an indication to provide better education and employment. Instead, a World Bank report shows that Africa performs poorly compared to youth education, as shown in Table 10.1. According to the World Bank, sub-Saharan Africa ranked the lowest in youth literacy globally.

Did the result above lead to education development to guarantee youths access to quality education. Instead, there are many obstacles to growth and access to education in Africa. These include poverty, conflicts, corruption, access to educational materials and infrastructure, governance, accountability, and mismanagement. These are the result of inadequate and weak leadership.

Table 10.1 Literacy rate, youth total (% of people aged **15–24)**

Country	*Percentage (%)*	*Year*
East Asia and the Pacific	99	2009
Europe and Central Asia	99	2009
Latin America and the Caribbean	97	2009
Middle East and North Africa	90	2009
Other small states	89	2009
South Asia	79	2009
Sub-Saharan Africa	72	2009
World	89	2009

Source: World Bank

Amid these challenges facing the youths, many in their secondary school age are heads of households in Africa, taking care of their siblings' economic and social well-being. Many of these youths who are heads of families at a very young age engage in economic activities for the upkeep of their households without support from the government or policy to take care of their vulnerabilities, except for South Africa, which has social grants for child-headed homes. It is at the age they should be in schools rather than being emboldened by adult life issues.

CHAPTER 11

Political Situation in Some African Countries

11.1 Nigeria

Nigeria is a country that comprises about two hundred and forty-two ethnic groups, and each ethnic group is distinct from the others in culture, language, and tradition. There is no problem with the Nigerian people, no problem with Nigeria's natural environment, and the country has numerous natural resources to sustain economic growth. Nigeria's problem since 1960 till date is weak leadership. Nigeria has always had leaders with good intentions. However, the destructive activities of bad leaders outweigh good leadership. Many Nigerians from different fields of life, in Nigeria and the diaspora, have argued that Nigeria as a nation is a pilot project by Britain that will never work. They cited continuous ethnic clashes due to different ethnic groups, religious zealots/differences, and a lack of patriotism. Some argue that Nigeria can be great, but because of poor accountability, lack of transparency, high corruption, and poor democratic development create the challenges it faces every day. Some believe that Nigeria's problem is enshrined in the structure of the country and the constitution. This group believes the constitution is weak and empowers dictatorial tendencies because it was written during the military era. I totally agree with all the factors mentioned. Nigeria's challenges are mixed bags that need urgent attention, or they break up.

C. E. Osuigwe, *Leadership and Economic Development Challenges in Post-Colonial Africa*, Sustainable Development Goals Series,
https://doi.org/10.1007/978-3-031-45663-3_11

Nigeria runs a federal system of government but does not operate like the USA federal system. Nigeria's resources are managed by the federal government, and states receive allocations from the federal government. Almost all the states in Nigeria look up to the federal government to function and implement their plans. The poor structure, the constitution coupled with weak leadership are the major problems of Nigeria since its independence up to the present.

Nigeria was granted independence on 1 October 1960. Since then, it has been rough socially and economically. The constitution in 1960 provided for a parliamentary system of government and a substantial measure of self-government for the country's four regions (the Northern, Eastern, Western, and Mid-Western Regions). The first black speaker of the Nigeria Parliament was Jaja Wachuku. He replaced Sir Frederick Metcalfe of the UK. Jaja Wachuku, as the Speaker of the House, received Nigeria's Instrument of Independence on 1 October 1960 from Princess Alexandra of Kent, the Queen's representative, at the independence ceremony. The post-independence political parties reflected the makeup of the three main ethnic groups and the regions. The Nigerian People's Congress (NPC) had more candidates from the Northern part, which was dominated by the Hausa-Fulani tribe, who were mainly Muslim. The National Convention of Nigerian Citizens (NCNC) was dominated by Igbos, mostly Christians from Eastern Nigeria. Action Group (AG) was dominated by the West, mainly Yoruba and mostly Muslims and Christians. The first national government was formed by the alliance of the NPC and NCNC. Sir Abubakar Tafawa Balewa from NPC was the prime minister, while Nnamdi Azikiwe of NCNC was the president. Under Chief Obafemi Awolowo's leadership, AG was the opposition party.

In January of 1966, six years after independence, Nigeria experienced its first military coup led by Chukwuma Kaduna Nzeogwu but could not succeed, and Aguyi Ironsi was appointed to lead Nigeria. In July 1966, Nigerian military officials led by Yakubu Gowon plotted a coup that killed Aguyi Ironsi and overthrew the government. Gowon took over the military leadership and government. The Eastern region was neglected and oppressed by the Gowon government. Because of the oppressive activities of Gowon in Eastern Nigeria, they agitated for a more liberal country, preferably a confederate state or a regional system with greater autonomy. The situation led to Aburi's negotiation in Ghana. During the Aburi intervention, the military leaders agreed to a confederate state. In Nigeria,

Yakubu Gowon reneged on the agreement and implemented centralised authority. Chinua Achebe captured what followed next succinctly:

> Beginning with the 15 January 1966 coup d'etat, through the countercoup (staged mainly by northern Nigerian Officers, who murdered 185 Igbo Officers) and the massacre of thirty thousand Igbos and Easterners in pogroms that started in May 1966 and occurred over four months—the events of those months left millions of other future Biafrans and me feeling terrified. As we fled "Home" to Eastern Nigeria to escape all the atrocities inflicted upon us and our families in different parts of Nigeria, we saw ourselves as victims. When we noticed that the federal government of Nigeria did not respond to our call to end pogroms, we concluded that a government that failed to safeguard the lives of its citizens has no claim to their allegiance and must be ready to accept that the victims deserve the right to seek safety in other ways—including secession. (Chinua Achebe 2012, p. 95)

The declaration of the Biafran State led to war. In less than one year in office, Yakubu Gowon was confronted with a civil war that lasted three years and ended in 1970. After the war, Gowon proclaimed a policy of 3Rs (Rehabilitation, Reconstruction, and Reintegration) for the Eastern Region to keep peace. Nevertheless, it was not implemented. Instead, Igbo people were incapacitated by seizing properties in all parts of Nigeria that were never returned. The properties were instead declared "abandoned properties". Every Igbo with a bank account or money saved at home before the war was given 20 pounds to start a new life, irrespective of the amount they had in their accounts or at home. The process disempowered the Igbo ethnic group as they began to fight for their economic space in Nigeria in 1970 and after.

Due to a lack of reconciliation and continued neglect and exploitation of Igbos since the end of the war, a new movement called the Movement for Actualization of the Sovereign State of Biafra (MASSOB) emerged in 1999 to agitate for an independent country for the Eastern part of Nigeria. Another movement, the Indigenous People of Biafra (IPOB), began around 2009 with the same goals as MASSOB. The lack of willingness of the Gowon leadership to step up a process to hand over to an elected democratic government led Murtala Mohammed to overthrow Gowon in the July 1975 coup. Murtala Mohammed promised public participation, respect for human rights, and a return to civilian rule. He emphasised the need for the return to a federal system of government. Murtala Muhammed's dream was short-lived. In February 1976, Buka Dumka overthrew Murtala Muhammed in a coup. The coup was unsuccessful. Murtala Muhammed was killed. The military leadership appointed Olusegun Obasanjo to lead the country and government. Obasanjo military regime raised students' school fees, banned student organisations, controlled workers' unions, nationalised land, and increased oil regulation.

Obasanjo's most outstanding military head-of-state achievement was returning power to civilian rule after three years. His achievement was overshadowed by the International Telephone and Telegraph (ITT) Corps project corruption, and more than 1 billion dollars went into the project without tangible success. Similarly, millions of dollars were spent on the FESTAC project without positive economic and social gains for the development of Nigeria and the suspected building of a private Ota farm with state money. Olusegun Obasanjo's military regime could be regarded as an emergency of full-blown corruption in Nigeria. Obasanjo military leadership conducted a democratic election in 1979 that brought in Shehu Shagari as the civilian president and Ifeanyichukwu Ekwueme as his deputy president. His period as a democratic president of Nigeria from 1979 to 1983 saw increased corruption and mismanagement of public funds. Shehu Shagari completed his first term as a civilian president and conducted elections in 1983, in which he won. The opposition parties complained that the election was rigged.

In December 1983, General Mohammadu Buhari overthrew Shehu Shagari's elected government, citing election rigging and corruption as excuses to overthrow the democratically elected government. Muhammadu Buhari promised to revive the country and wipe out corruption. He promised to hand over governance to a democratically elected government as quickly as possible. His promises were not different news from those made by former military leaders as they came to power through coups. Buhari suppressed criticism against the government and constrained the freedom of the press. He banned many organisations and declared a War against Indiscipline to deal with public behaviour, public appearance, corruption, smuggling, and laziness in public institutions and government departments and to enhance patriotism. He initiated austerity measures that made it difficult for some companies to operate. It led to inflation and economic hardship. Military personnel broke into private warehouses and businesses, selling goods at giveaway prices. The adversities that ensued led to dissatisfaction and frustration among Nigerians.

On 27 August 1985, Ibrahim Babangida overthrew Muhammadu Buhari in a military coup. Ibrahim Babangida described Muhammadu

Buhari as insensitive to Nigerians' feelings and the primary reason he overthrew him. Babangida projected an image of a human rights activist, and this faded within a short period. However, to his credit, he released many politicians detained by Muhammadu Buhari since 1983. He developed economic reforms that led Nigeria into more financial crises. Due to the persistence of economic problems and galloping food prices, there was a failed coup attempt led by Mamman Vatsa, and he was executed along with his fellow coup plotters. On 22 April 1990, there was another failed coup led by Gideon Orkar, and he was executed with some of his coup plotters while others could escape. The recurring coup plotting led Babangida's emergency exit from Lagos, the former Nigeria capital, to Abuja for security reasons. In 1990, Ibrahim Babangida reviewed the constitution of Nigeria and planned to return Nigeria to the elected government. In 1993, he conducted another election, which local and international observers said to be free and fair. Moshood Abiola was declared the winner, but Babangida annulled the elections. The annulment of the elections led to protests and riots. People were killed, and properties were destroyed. Human rights activists and journalists were arrested, and some opposition newspapers were banned. International and domestic pressures were mounted on Babangida's military government, and he resigned and formed an interim government headed by Ernest Shonekan in August 1993. The interim government aimed to conduct a fresh election within six months.

Shonekan's interim government did not last up to six months in office. In November 1993, Sani Abacha, a military leader, overthrew the interim government. Sani Abacha was Babangida's defence minister. Abacha dismantled democratic institutions as well as the elected National and State Assemblies. He banned all political activities and suspended the constitution. Within this period, Moshood Abiola, who won the 1993 election, proclaimed himself president of Nigeria. Sani Abacha arrested him and put him in jail on charges of treason. Many political and democratic activists were arrested, and many fled from Nigeria for fear of their lives. In October 1995, Sani Abacha announced a two-year transitional plan to bring Nigeria to an elected democratic government. The growing frustration and anger at the military tactics of the Abacha regime led to the Lawan Gwadaba coup, in which Olusengu Obasanjo and Shehu Musa Yar' Adua (the senior brother of the Nigerian president between 2007–2009) were implicated. The people who were involved in the coup were imprisoned for 25 years.

Yar'Adua died in prison, and Obasanjo remained in jail throughout Abacha's regime.

Abacha schemed to become an elected president of Nigeria or to elongate his power. According to Abacha's military report, in December 1997, a failed coup was plotted by Oladipo Diya, Sani Abacha's second-in-command. In 1998, Diya and his four partners in the coup plot were sentenced to death while other participants in the attempted coup were imprisoned. Fortunately for Diya and other coup plotters, they were not killed before Abacha died on 8 June 1998. Moshood Abiola, the winner of the 1993 democratic election, died in July 1998.

What started as a ruffle of shoulders my military personals in 1966 turned Nigeria into a flea market. Most of the military officials were intoxicated with power and greed. Within the flea market, what could be heard was noise, nothing but noise, the noise of people intoxicated with the ability to rule and suppress. In the flea market, decisions and policies were made for Nigerians. That was Nigeria in the hands of the military till 1999, from the first coup in 1966.

The death of Sani Abacha and Moshood Abiola led to the appointment of Abdusalam Abubakar as Nigeria's military head and president. In a short period, Abdusalam Abubakar conducted elections that former military leader Olusegun Obasanjo won under the People's Democratic Party. He was brought out of prison to contest the election. The emergence of a democratic government led by Obasanjo brought more hope and opened economic opportunities. However, there were challenges to accountability and transparency. The economic opportunities attracted foreign investments and increased domestic investments. Obasanjo failed in the electoral process and an assumption that he attempted to amend the constitution to allow for a third term in office.

In 2007, a general election brought Umaru Yar'Adua and Goodluck Jonathan of PDP as president and vice president, respectively. The international and local observers condemned the elections for the second time in a row, saying they were marred by fraud and irregularities. In November 2009, Yar'Adua was flown out of Nigeria to Saudi Arabia for medical treatment. Due to his extended hospitalization, in February 2010, Goodluck Jonathan began acting as president in the absence of Umaru Yar'Adua, who later died in May 2010. The president's death led Goodluck Jonathan to serve as the president for the remaining tenure of Umaru Yar'Adua. In April 2011, Goodluck Jonathan conducted elections in which he stood as president candidate under PDP and won.

Goodluck Jonathan's government succeeded in some sectors, such as rehabilitating national roads. The agricultural policy improved farming and contributed up to 25% of the GDP. Some interstate rail lines that have not been functional for more than three decades were rehabilitated, and some were in the rehabilitation process. Similarly, for more than two decades, there was no activity in the auto assembly industry in Nigeria. Many of the country's airports received a good facelift as infrastructure and facilities within the airports were rehabilitated. Access to petroleum products improved. There was also an increase in electricity generation and distribution. Jonathan also established 12 more federal universities so that every state in Nigeria could have at least one federal university and to create greater access to university education. However, there were challenges in sustaining a good standard of education in Nigeria. Under Jonathan's leadership, Nigeria became Africa's first destination for foreign investments. After rebasing the economic status of the country in 2013, the country came out as the biggest economy in Africa. Despite the success of Goodluck Jonathan, his government battled with corruption and insecurity.

In March 2015, Jonathan conducted presidential elections in which he stood as the presidential candidate of the People's Democratic Party (PDP), and his primary opponent was Muhammadu Buhari of the All-Progressive Congress (APC). Buhari won the election. Domestic and international observers applauded the elections and congratulated the president for conducting free and fair elections. In his broadcast to the country after the elections, Jonathan addressed his countrymen as follows:

> "Fellow Nigerians, thank you for turning out in-masse for the 28 March General Elections. I promised the country free and fair elections. I have kept my word. I have also expanded the space for Nigerians to participate in the democratic process. That is one legacy I would like to see endure". "As I have always affirmed, nobody's ambition is worth the blood of any Nigerian. The unity, stability and progress of our dear country is more important than anything else. I congratulate all Nigerians for successfully going through the process of the March 28th General Elections with the commendable enthusiasm and commitment that was demonstrated nationwide". "I have conveyed my personal best wishes to General Muhammadu Buhari. May God Almighty continue to bless the Federal Republic of Nigeria".

Goodluck Jonathan became the first president to concede defeat in elections in Nigeria's history. This action was expected to enhance democratic values in Nigeria and Africa. With the improvement in democracy and free and fair elections under Goodluck Ebele Jonathan, there was an expectation from Buhari to continue to improve on the achievements of Jonathan. However, the hope disappeared within a short period. Since 29 May 2015, Nigeria has slipped from being the number one destination for foreign investments in Africa to the recession, where millions lost their jobs, many companies left the country, and many investments closed. Many Nigerians who voted for Buhari in the hope that he would fight corruption that had bedevilled Nigeria for more than five decades lost hope as corruption escalated. In the last five years, there have been many reports on corrupt cases of political elites and civil servants, but the government is dragging their feet in initiating cases against these corrupt individuals. Examples of such issues as reported in Premium Times newspaper on 21 January 2019 by Sani Tukur in the article "Atiku Releases List of Corrupt Buhari Associates" were the following: Abba Kyari's N500m bribe allegation from MTN / N29.9m contract scam, Babachir Lawal (sacked SGF) who benefitted from corruption scandal about cutting of grass at refugee camps in North East of Nigeria, Bola Tinubu's Alpha Beta on N100b corruption case, Chief of Army Staff, Lt. Gen. Tukur Buratai: Allegedly bought 2 Dubai mansions for $1.5m, The First Lady, Aisha Mohamadu reported her ADC, Sani Baban-Inna, to the security agencies over allegation of swindling members of the public of the sum of N2.5b, nothing came out of it, Senator Hadi Sirika (N1.2b Nigeria Air fraud scandal). Ojoye (2018) states, "At least eight out of the politicians working for the re-election of President Muhammadu Buhari in the February 2019 election have pending corruption cases worth N232bn, checks by *Saturday PUNCH* have revealed. Investigation by our correspondents showed that the amount involved in the various graft cases, which are currently pending before security agencies, especially the Economic and Financial Crimes Commission, range from N223m to N100bn for each of the politicians". It was why the elected government of Buhari was unable to fight corruption and hold corrupt officials accountable. It was a disaster from the onset. Similarly, the 11 March 2023 presidential election was one of the worst elections conducted in Nigeria's history. It was mired with conflicts, ethnic tension, and corruption.

The actions of many political elites in Nigeria are tantamount to waging war against true democracy. These acts include rigging elections and instigating violence and intimidation of voters when they lose elections or realise they cannot win any election. The systematic oppression of the electorate during elections was institutionalised to create atmospheres of fear and chaos to rig elections under such circumstances. This electoral violence is unleashed through ethnic clashes and sometimes the use of security agencies.

Antonio Maria Costa (2007), the Executive Director of the Vienna-based United Nations Office on Drugs and Crimes, said, "Nigeria used to be synonymous with corruption just a few years ago. Unscrupulous leaders pilfered the national coffers and stashed away billions of dollars in foreign bank accounts. By some estimates, nearly US $400 billion was stolen between 1960 and 1999. Sani Abacha alone is estimated to have stolen the equivalent of 2–3 per cent of the country's GDP every year he was President. That is a staggering—almost 'astronomical'—amount of money because if you were to put 400-billion-dollar bills end-to-end, you could make 75 round trips to the moon! Concretely, those 400 billion dollars could have translated into millions of vaccinations for children; thousands of kilometres of roads; hundreds of schools, hospitals and water treatment facilities that never came to be" (Costa 2007). Summarising Obasanjo's civilian regime (1999–2007), Pa Enahoro described it as a country run as a unitary system, split into military cantonments, battalions, and platoons, with an ultra-powerful centre. He pointed out that we have unviable states that cannot survive without handouts from the central government. Pa Enahoro indicated that Nigerians must do away with emotions on the current grave issues confronting the country, that for more than 35 years Nigeria was run like a vehicle with a drunken driver loaded with reckless passengers urging the driver to drive on. Pa Enahoro described the election that replaced President Obasanjo as a naïve kid. Imagine where the losers of elections were called by pacifists to go to the election tribunals. He questioned whether the judiciary should be burdened by electoral crimes deliberately committed by members of the executive and legislative arms of government, egged on by their patrons and godfathers. He stated that members of the judiciary are not miracle workers. To ask the court to resolve the obscene violations of electoral processes blatantly displayed by political agents in the last general elections is like asking a physician to raise the dead from the grave.

Since 1980, there have been more than five Nigerian economic visions. A society will only have a vision upon vision without analysing why the previous visions failed. With understanding the failure of the last visions, the 2020 vision will succeed because what led to the failure of prior visions will also lead to the failure of Vision 2020. As indicated, Vision 2020 failed, and another vision will replace it. Leadership needs to be improved, not the plans and strategies mapped out on these numerous visions.

Nigeria is deeply divided along numerous lines and cleavages: ethnicity, religion, and even regional lines. It is a country where citizens can only aspire to contest elections and hold elective offices in a state if they are indigenes. The exception is Lagos State, where sometimes non-indigenes break this trend to compete and win elections because of the tribal diversity in Lagos. It is a country where a citizen finds it difficult to get a job in a local and state government if he or she is not an indigene of that state. Even the delivery of justice is divided along socio-economic lines. It is a country where a leader embezzled more than 1 billion naira (1.3 million dollars) from the pension fund, was found guilty, and sentenced to pay a fine of 700,000 naira (900 dollars). He walks free. In the same month, an ordinary citizen was convicted and sentenced to six years' imprisonment for stealing a goat. It is a state hijacked by a few political elites and leaders.

My suggestion regarding these challenges is to restructure Nigeria to a regional system of government. Some people have argued that Nigeria's structure is not the problem but leadership. I agree with them, but for Nigeria to be sustainable both economically and socially, a regional system like that of the UK and UAE is the best option for Nigeria where the six regions (South-South, Southeast, Southwest, North Central, Northwest, and Northeast) are semi-autonomous with a weak central government. This will stimulate healthy competition at all levels and all spheres. A restructured Nigeria will unleash hard work, innovations, and economic growth. This form of government will make optimal use of resources for the benefit of its citizens. For Nigeria to develop sustainably, there should be an outright war against corruption. The government should allocate more funds towards infrastructural development than the rate it has been doing since the 1960s. Private/Public participation in infrastructural development should be promoted to speed delivery, and civil servants should be orientated in delivering their services in Nigeria. Ethics and professionalism in infrastructure and service delivery should be upheld. Nigeria needs to improve its public health and education system. More budgets should be allocated to education and health, ensuring they are implemented transparently and are accountable.

11.2 South Africa

The quest for good governance, integrated development, and inclusivity since the oppressive apartheid government surrendered power to a democratic government in South Africa is promising. There has been good improvement in access to housing, less racial society, and more access to service delivery. However, there are incidents of corruption. Similarly, many municipalities' financials, budgetary allocation, and implementation of projects are challenging. Some provincial government departments have been under supervision by the national government. Consequently, a lot must be done to avoid what is happening in other African countries, particularly concerning corruption, cult-figure leadership, ethnic tension, and leadership with dictatorial tendencies.

The African people's struggle in South Africa was long and painful. They fought the apartheid system, policies, and strategies to ensure its oppressive apartheid government was dislodged. The battle led to the formation of the ANC. According to the ANC website, in 1912, chiefs, representatives of people and church organisations, and other prominent individuals gathered in Bloemfontein and formed the African National Congress. The ANC declared its aim to unite all Africans as one people to defend their rights and freedoms. Before the formation of ANC, the vital force against the apartheid government was the Industrial and Commercial Workers Union (ICU). Due to the non-sustainability of the union, it died off in the late 1920s.

In 1940, the ANC agitated for the rights of black people and started exploring the necessity for militant action against the oppressive apartheid government. In 1944, the ANC Youth League was formed, and Nelson Mandela, Oliver Tambo, and Walter Sisulu became the first youth league leaders. The formation of the youth league led to the mobilisation of youth for military struggle.

ANC and many organisations stood firm against the Group Areas Act, Bantu Education Act, and Population Registration Act. In the 1950s, the youth league resistance campaign against the apartheid government expanded to include the involvement of the South Africa Indian Congress, the South Africa Coloured People Organization (SACPO), and the Congress of Democrats (COD) to cooperate in campaigning against the racist laws and rules of the apartheid government. During this period, SACTU, ANC, and other organisations formed the Congress Alliance.

In 1955, the apartheid government initiated implementing a pass law to travel to major cities in South Africa, leading to women's protests. The South African chiefs' collaboration caused the Pondoland revolt during this period. The revolt was one of the noticeable rural agitations against the apartheid government. The chiefs demanded an end to Bantu education and tax and to be represented in the government. During the same period, PAC steered a crusade that led to Sharpville homicide by the apartheid government, and the apartheid government shot unarmed protesters and killed 69 South Africans.

In 1961, the ANC took up arms against the South African Government because the peaceful protests and the subsequent banning of the ANC alone would not force the regime to change. The ANC went underground and formed Umkhonto we Sizwe (MK) to fight to defend black people, their future, and their freedom. Within the period, the apartheid government passed a law for the death penalty for sabotage and allowed police to detain people for 90 days without trial. The rules led to a police raid at MK's headquarters and MK leadership's arrest, leading to the Rivonia trial. To an extent, the Rivonia trial incapacitated the ANC's functions and capabilities.

In 1976, students' frustration grew against Bantu education, and they protested in several parts of South Africa. It resulted in the killing of thousands of South Africans, including Hector Pertersen. The students' uprising increased the number of Umkhonto WeSizwe (MK) members. In the 1980s, the apartheid government secret unit killed many activists, bombed their homes, and declared a state of emergency in some areas. The state of emergency was used as cover to arrest many people. The SADF raided many neighbouring African countries to fight ANC and other anti-apartheid organisations. The 1980s also witnessed the rise of many organisations, the United Democratic Front and Congress of South African Students (COSAS), and the new organisations geared up against the apartheid government policies. The formation of COSATU in 1985 drew other workers' organisations together against government policies on wages and benefits.

Furthermore, the ANC called for township resistance. The aim was to destroy Black Local Authorities. Black officials, police, and councillors were asked to resign from their posts. Many apartheid government partners were attacked, leading to a total breakdown of apartheid rule in townships.

The protests and periodic planned attacks put pressure on the apartheid government. With internal and external pressure from the international community, the apartheid government unbanned ANC in 1990. They also noted their interest in bringing back the peaceful co-existence of all races in South Africa. In 1991, Nelson Mandela was elected president at the ANC National Conference, and Oliver Tambo was the national chairperson; in 1994, Nelson Mandela became the first black president in democratic South Africa.

ANC is one of the oldest political parties in Africa and the world. Its members were imprisoned, tortured, and killed for almost a century. It overcame all forces of apartheid. As a party, it has held the majority support of South African people since its formation and has integrated all South African ethnic groups. The idea of influence in the ANC is good. However, the number of cliques in the present ANC needs to be revised to maintain the objectives, ideology, and philosophy on which the party was founded. The worst aspect of the cliques is that they are based on the quest for financial gain and political influence rather than social and economic justice and equity. There is nothing wrong with having cliques in a political party, provided that the cliques are for political and economic ideology, not selfish purposes.

ANC, for years, had good leadership with clear-cut goals and vision. The party provided the manpower needed to run a smooth government in 1994. From 2011 till 2023, the ANC has become obsessed with the issue of leadership. It is problematic when people start philosophising that revolutions are about individual and clique goals and visions rather than society's goals. Revolution is about force or protests and a drastic positive change that needs favourable policies and legislation to encourage social and economic development and transformation. A revolution is also about the society and its people's willingness to peacefully challenge undemocratic and undevelopable ideals in the community. It involves awareness and empowerment. It is not about killing a person or a group of persons against society's goals and vision.

Democratic Alliance (DA) as a party has flaws in its internal politics. There have been complaints about how leaders are picked. To many South Africans, the DA is a white party trying to show off some black faces in their leadership structure to garner black votes during elections. Even though DA seems to present a unified front, there is a need for internal democracy to take root in the party for it to emerge as a party comprising different races. DA's former president, Helen Zille, was quoted to have said that blacks from South Africa who "migrated" from other provinces to Western Cape were "refugees". The same Helen Zille made a statement justifying colonisation and only apologised to those offended by her comment. DA could have shown Helen Zille the door from the first time she called Black South Africans in Cape Town refugees.

Economic Freedom Party (EFF) ideology as a party is based on a radical economic approach to social and economic development. EFF strongly believes in pushing for black ownership of resources and government control of specific institutions. They also stated in their 2019 election manifesto that they would have only two ties of government, the national and local governments. It should not be said that EFF is a new child on the block; it has emerged as one of the most vigorous oppositions in South Africa. However, as a political party, it is only discipline and courage with an excellent internal political party democracy that will make them a strong opposition or possible ruling party.

In trying to maintain internal discipline, some parties have trampled on democratic principles and tended towards some sort of totalitarianism or cult followership. For example, the Inkatha Freedom Party (IFP) saw its support dwindle because of a lack of democratic principles within the party structure and internal elections. Mongosuthu Buthelezi has led IFP for more than 30 years. COPE was a promising party, but the power struggle within the party portrayed the party in a negative image to the electorate. South Africa should be one of the countries that should lead by example through sound democratic principles in Africa.

11.3 Ivory Coast

Ivory Coast was one of the most peaceful countries in Africa pre-1999. The country thrived on agriculture development before the breakout of conflict. It is a country where many beverage companies worldwide source cocoa to produce their products. It was a meeting place for many ECOWAS citizens. From 1999 till 2012, Ivory Coast failed to have peace because of conflict. The conflict impacted Ivory Coast's agricultural sector and social and economic development and integration.

The former president of Ivory Coast, Félix Houphouët-Boigny, founded the first agriculture trade union in 1944 and was the first president of Ivory Coast at independence on 7 August 1960. From 1960 to 1993, he ruled under a one-party state Democratic Party of Ivory Coast as the official party, and opposition parties were banned. In 1990,

Houphouet-Boigny was pressured to support multiparty democracy after thousands of civil servants went on strike with students protesting against institutional corruption. The protest led to multiparty democracy. Introducing a multiparty system led to the election in which Felix Houphouet-Boigny contested and defeated Laurent Gbagbo, the Ivorian Popular Front (IPF) political leader.

In 1993, Houphouet-Boigny died and was succeeded by Mr Henri Konan Bedie, president of the national assembly. Henri Bedie introduced the policy of "Ivorite", meaning Ivory Coast for Ivory Coast indigenes. Many Ivorian citizens originate from bordering African countries, and either or both of their parents come from neighbouring ECOWAS member countries. Ivorite denied many Ivorians their citizenship, which led to ethnic tension. The tension led to Ivorian conflicts initiated by an African leader, destroying a peaceful and buoyant agro-based social and economic system.

In 1995, Ivory Coast held a presidential election, and Konan Bedie won. The opposition parties boycotted the election, citing restrictions imposed on their candidates. For example, Ouattara's nomination was ruled invalid by the "Ivorite" policy and was excluded from the election because of the assumption that his father was from Burkina Faso. Konan Bedie's Workers Party provided an illusion of parliamentary contestation, and he declared himself president by almost 96% of the votes. It allowed him to tighten his grip on power and jailed hundreds of opposition supporters.

In late 1999, Konan Henri Bedie fled to France in exile when he was overthrown in a military coup led by General Robert Guei. The new leader pressed for austerity measures and openly campaigned for a less wasteful Ivory Coast. General Guei conducted general elections in October 2000 in which Laurent Gbagbo vied with Robert Guei. The lead-up to the election was marked by conflicts, civil unrest, and public uprising that led to about 180 deaths. Robert Guei declared himself the winner of the election and proclaimed himself president. The declaration of Robert Guei as president led to a popular uprising, and Robert Guei left the country, and Laurent Gbagbo replaced him. Also, the Supreme Court of Ivory Coast disqualified Alassane Ouattara from contesting in the election of October 2000 for the second time because of the Ivorite Policy.

The disqualification of Alassane Ouattara created tension after the election. In September 2002, while the former president (Laurent Gbagbo) was out of the country, an armed uprising started. Armed troops, mainly from the Northern part of Ivory Coast, launched attacks in many cities. The rebels took control of the Northern Ivory Coast with a stronghold in the north of the town of Bouake. The deployment of French troops stopped the rebels from re-launching an attack in Abidjan after their first attempt to get hold of the city failed. In 2003, Laurent Gbagbo and rebel leaders signed an agreement that created a "government of national unity". In 2004, the relationship between Laurent Gbagbo and the opposition deteriorated, and the national unity government failed. The unity government's failure led to the killing of protesters, many foreign nationals were evacuated, and UN peacekeepers were deployed to maintain a Zone of Confidence.

In November 2004, the peace agreement collapsed because the rebel groups refused to disarm. President Gbagbo ordered airstrikes against the rebels' stronghold in Bouake, during which nine French soldiers were killed. The Ivorian government apologised for killing the French soldiers, claiming it was a mistake. On the other hand, the French government insisted that it was a deliberate action.

In October 2005, Gbagbo's presidential term expired. Due to the lack of disarmament of the rebels, the African Union brokered an extension of his presidential term office by one year, and the United Nations Security Council approved the plan. Political manoeuvrings led Laurent Gbagbo to stay in power till the 2010 general election. The preliminary results announced by the Electoral Commission showed a loss for Gbagbo in favour of Alassane Ouattara. The ruling Front Populaire Ivoirien (FPI) contested the outcome of the election before the Constitutional Council, claiming massive fraud in the Northern part of Ivory Coast that was controlled by the rebels known as Forces Nouvelles de Cote d'Ivoire (FNCI). Constitutional Council declared the results of the election in most of the Northern Ivory Coast as illegitimate and declared Laurent Gbagbo the winner of the election with 51% of the vote cast, instead of Alassane Ouattara, who scored 54%, as reported by the Electoral Commission.

The international community condemned the action of the Constitutional Council, upheld the result of the Electoral Commission, and acknowledged Alassane Ouattara as the winner of the 2010 election. These circumstances led to an outbreak of war in Ivory Coast. African Union sent the former president of South Africa (Thabo Mbeki) to arbitrate on the conflict, but it failed. ECOWAS and the African Union suspended Ivory Coast from their memberships. The conflict entered a critical stage after many failed resolutions, unsuccessful peace negotiations, and sporadic violence. Forces loyal to Ouattara seized control of many parts of the country, while Gbagbo was trapped in Abidjan, the capital of Ivory Coast. Many people were killed, and thousands fled the country during the conflicts. International organisations reported many cases of human rights violations by forces supporting both Ouattara and Gbagbo. On 10 April 2011, Laurent Gbagbo was captured inside his residence in Abidjan.

The origin of Ivory Coast's conflicts was the amendment of the country's constitution, which stipulates that for a person to contest an election in Ivory Coast, he must be born in Ivory Coast with parents who were/are indigenes of Ivory Coast. If Ivory Coast leadership or almost all African leaders and political elites were French that elected Nicolas Sarkozy, whose father is from Hungary (Pál Sárközy de Nagy-Bócsa), they could have told the masses that elected him to go to hell, or they would have engaged in acts that will bring down the economy. Three Nigerians, Chuka Ummuna, Helen Grant, and Chi Onwurah, contested the UK general elections and emerged victorious, winning seats in the British parliament. The British prime minister in October 2022, Rishi Sunak, whose parents are from Eastern Africa but with Indian heritage, could not have been PM of Britain. If Africa's leaders and political elites were Americans in California who elected a European immigrant, Arnold Schwarzenegger, as their governor, they could have turned California upside down. If Africa's leaders and political elites were Americans, they could not have allowed Obama to contest an election, not even a councillor election, because his father was from Africa. African leaders often polarised society for selfish gains that promoted mediocrity instead of merit.

All the ringleaders of the conflicts in Ivory Coast used ethnicity and religion as an instrument to manipulate the poor, uneducated, and frustrated citizens in pursuit of their selfish and greedy agendas. The main reason for plunging the Ivory Coast into conflict is the policy of "Ivorite", which was initiated to sideline people with non-Ivorian parental backgrounds. The policy became an instrument for human rights abuse, insecurity, and social and economic underdevelopment.

11.4 DR Congo (DRC)

Many African countries were "baptised" with independence in 1960. It was the same year that DRC got its independence from Belgium, and Patrice Lumumba was the president. Lumumba was assassinated in 1961, and Mobutu Sese Soko became the DRC president. It seems the baptism of 1960 was also the baptism of conflict that surged in the 1990s. The conflict in DRC was regional destruction, which involved nine African countries and rendered the development of the region and that of DRC ineffective and displaced millions of DRC citizens and the neighbouring countries. The genocide in Rwanda also contributed to the DRC conflict because of ethnic patronage. The Rwandan conflict split over to DRC in 1996 when the Rwandan Hutu Interahamwe Rebels fled Rwanda following the takeover of the Rwanda government by new leadership and started using Hutu refugee camps in Eastern DRC as a base for incursions against Rwanda. The use of DRC as a base for an attack against the Rwandan government by Interahamwe prompted Rwandan troops (RPA) and the Ugandan Army to enter DRC as part of an armed coalition led by Laurent-Desire Kabila, known as the Alliance des Forces Democratiques pour la Liberation du Congo-Zaire (AFDL). AFDL forcibly ousted Mobuto Sese Seko from power, and Laurent Kabila declared himself president. A year after toppling the government of Sese Seko, in 1997, the relations between Laurent Kabila and his foreign backers weakened, and he ordered all foreign troops in DRC to leave, and some of the forces refused to leave.

On 16 January 2001, one of his bodyguards assassinated Laurent Kabila, and his son Joseph Kabila replaced him. In 2002, a peace symposium involving most rebel groups was held in South Africa. By April 2003, much progress was made at the peace conference in Pretoria, and Joseph Kabila selected four vice presidents for the transitional government he headed. He promised to hold an election between 2005 and 2006. Despite the peace agreement, conflicts continued and claimed lives in Eastern DRC.

An estimated more than 1 million people were killed during more than ten years of the conflict. UN deployed up to 20 thousand troops to DRC, and the war consumed more than 1 billion dollars a year. If 1 billion dollars were poured into the DRC economy every year for the past ten years without conflict, what would the economy of DRC look like? Who are the architects of the DRC conflict? Many people might accuse Western individuals of seeking blood money from solid mineral resources, but how many of their faces did you see in the war? It is political elites' and leaders' greediness. Can you be paid to destroy your family? Can I pay you to kill those whom you are supposed to protect? Can I pay you so I can take the bread or food to keep your children alive? Can I pay you to rob you of what is so dear to you? Can I pay you to take your dignity away? Can I pay you to render your children useless? What can I give you to destroy what will keep your family alive for generations to come? By answering these questions, we may come to terms with the solution to what is happening in DRC and who to blame. DRC needs a holistic solution to their problems. The answer needs reconciliation, political stability, and social and economic empowerment. Would the government of Felix Tshisekedi shave ethnicity and work with all for the benefit of DRC citizens? Or will he be another African leader who will fail to do the right things for the use of its citizens, not the few stakeholders that assisted in bringing him to power?

11.5 Sudan

Sudan has the most enormous landmass in Africa and two broad racial backgrounds, which are African and Arab origin. The independence of Sudan ushered in a five-member Sovereignty Council with rival nationalist agendas with no clear leadership. Freedom witnessed one of the deadliest conflicts in Africa between North and South (1956–1972 and 1983–2005) and in Darfur. In 1958, two years after the independence, General Ibrahim Abboud overthrew the Sovereignty Council that led the country and institutionalised Islamic systems and policies. By 1964, Sudan was deeply divided into Arab Muslim North and Christian South of Sudan. There was heavy discrimination against the Southern Sudanese. The discrimination led to the uprising that ousted General Abboud in 1964. Between 1964 and 1969, a period of five years, four presidents ruled Sudan. They include the following:

1. Sirr Al-Khatim Al-Khalifa: 1 October and second transitional governments 1964–1965
2. Muhammad Ahmed Mahgoub: 1965 to 1966 and 1967 to 1969
3. Sadig AlMahdi: 1966 to 1967 and
4. Babiker Awadalla; May 1969 to October 1969.

After a series of presidents, in 1969, Gaafar Muhammad an-Nimeriy gained power through a coup d'état. In 1971, a failed Communist coup left Nimeriy politically isolated, forcing him to seek peace with Ethiopia, Uganda, and Southern Sudanese rebels. At Addis Ababa in Ethiopia in March 1972, a peace agreement was reached with Anya-Nya. Southern Sudan was granted autonomy and became a self-governing region, and the guerrillas were integrated into the army.

The systematic and organised violations of the agreement by the Northern dominated Sudanese government, combined with an increase in Islamic shift in the late 1970s and the discovery of oil in the South, ultimately led to a resumption of hostilities against Southern Sudan and the deployment of Northern troops to the Southern oil-rich region. Following the mutiny by Southern troops against the government in early 1983, President Nimeriy revoked the Addis Ababa agreement, dissolved the South's constitutional guarantees, and declared Arabic the official language of Sudan. Three months later, Islamic Sharia law replaced the traditional Sudanese law. The hostility of President Nimeriy to Southern Sudan led to the formation of an armed liberation group called Sudan People's Liberation Army/Movement (SPLA/M), directed by John Garang. SPLA/M activities led to a popular uprising that led to the overthrow of Nimeriy in 1985. In 1986, Sadiq al-Mahdi's democratic government (Umma Party) was elected president. Sadiq al-Mahdi's move towards peace between the SPLA/M and the government was stalled when the National Islamic Front (NIF) led a bloodless coup in June 1989, a day before a bill to suspend Sharia law was to be passed. NIF was led by General Omar al-Bashir. NIF transformed into a political party called the National Congress Party (NCP). General Omar al-Bashir revoked the constitution, barred opposition parties, moved to Islamize the judicial, and stepped up the North-South war.

In March 2005, the United Nations Security Council (UNSC) referred the Darfur matter to the International Criminal Court. The court issued a warrant of arrest against the Janjaweed commander and President Omar al-Bashir for war crimes and genocide. To ease economic problems in Sudan, in 2017, the USA lifted some sanctions on Sudan. It did not help the financial situation; in November 2018, inflation hit 70%, and the Sudanese pound plummeted in value. Al-Bashir imposed emergency austerity measures and cut fuel and bread subsidies. The cut in subsidies triggered mass protests nationwide in December, leading to demand for Bashir to step down.

During the protest, more than 1000 protesters were reportedly detained by government forces. However, Mr Bashir was defiant and declared a state of emergency, dismissed the federal government, and replaced all state governors with members of the security forces. He tried to appease protesters, saying he would step down at the end of his term in April 2020. The protesters continued and argued he had previously pledged to step down and reneged. After long anti-government protests, a military council led by Lieutenant General Abdel Fattah al-Burhan removed Al-Bashir from power and oversaw a transitional period of two years. However, protesters demanded that the army ruler should hand over immediately to a civilian-led transitional government. After lengthy negotiations, 11 individuals in the Sovereign Council were appointed to lead a transitional government headed by Prime Minister Abdalla Hamdok for three years to ensure a democratically elected government. Within three years, it was expected that the transitional government will be able to set economic and security plans to repair a damaged country by its former leaders.

Nevertheless, in 2023, another conflict reared its ugly head. The Sudan conflict was one of the longest wars in the world that involved neighbouring countries such as Eritrea and Ethiopia and affected the economic growth and integration of the region. Sudan is a nation of perambulation with no genuine social and economic direction. Due to weak leadership, Sudan's conflict has claimed more than 1.5 million citizens since its independence.

11.6 Uganda

Uganda became independent in 1962, and the first prime minister was Milton Obote. At the onset of independence, like in Nigeria, ethnic politicking became the norm that distorted the idea of sustainable governance and development. In 1963, Uganda became a republic with Buganda King Edward Mutesa as the president and Milton Obote as the prime minister. In 1966, a power tussle and political manoeuvring between Milton Obote and King Edward Mutesa reached a climax, and Prime Minister Milton Obote stripped off all the powers from the Buganda King and promoted himself to the position of president. In 1967, a new constitution was promulgated, which vested more power to the president and abolished the Buganda kingdom. The relationship between the Buganda king, Edward Mutesa 11 and Obote deteriorated. Obote sent a force led by Idi Amin to attack Kabaka palace, and King Edward Mutesa fled to Britain.

In 1971, di Amin Dada ousted Milton Obote from power through a coup and declared himself "president". Idi Amin dissolved parliament and declared himself life president with absolute power. He claimed part of Kenya and had a border conflict with Tanzania. In 1978, Idi Amin invaded Tanzania to annex the Kagera region and sent away the Asian immigrants in Uganda. He killed and sidelined many oppositions, particularly those not from his ethnic group or ethnic groups who did not support his leadership. Over a hundred thousand Ugandans who did not belong to Amin's tribe were tortured or murdered during his eight-year reign.

In 1979, Tanzania invaded Uganda and unified various rebel groups under the Uganda National Liberation Front and ousted Idi Amin's leadership, and he fled to Libya. An interim government led by Yusuf Lule was formed. In June 1979, following a dispute over the extent of presidential powers, Yusuf Lule was replaced with Godfrey Binaisa. In 1980, Binaisa was removed from power through a military coup chaired by Paulo Muwanga.

In December 1980, elections were conducted, and the Uganda People's Congress (UPC) came to power under the leadership of President Milton Obote, with Paulo Muwanga as vice president. In December 1980, Yoweri Museveni's National Resistance Army (NRA) rebel group came into force and killed many innocent citizens. Similarly, Milton Obote abused human rights in the fight to destroy the stronghold of Yoweri Museveni. In July 1985, Lt General Bazilio Olara-Okello ousted Obote from the government, and Milton Obote fled to exile in Zambia.

Gen. Bazilio Olara-Okello negotiated with Museveni's rebels' group (NRA) and guaranteed to improve human rights, conduct free and fair elections, and end tribal animosity. General Bazilio Okello failed to adhere to his pledge and continued a brutal insurgency against the Yoweri Museveni rebel group (NRA). In 1985, Okello and Yoweri Museveni went to Kenya for negotiations under the arbitration of President Daniel Arap Moi, seeking a ceasefire and a coalition government. They agreed on a truce, but NRA continued fighting. In 1986 Okello's government fell when Museveni and his rebel group seized Kampala and the country. The rebel group formed a government with Museveni as president.

In 2005, the Ugandan parliament, controlled by Museveni, approved a constitutional amendment that scrapped presidential term limits. Since the constitution modification that scraped the presidential limit in the office, Yoweri Museveni won all presidential elections in Uganda despite the high mismanagement of resources and corruption. The year 2023 marked the year that Yoweri Museveni has ruled Uganda for 37 years. The challenge in Uganda is enormous. Not only does Uganda have its problems, but the involvement of Uganda in other countries' conflicts through rebel groups is impacting the development of the country and the region. Like in many other African countries, ethnicity played a significant role in the conflicts in Uganda. It was known that colonial masters brought many ethnic groups together for their effective administration and business interests. However, many of these ethnic groups have failed to function in diversity. A strategy is needed to make African countries embrace ethnic diversity for sustainable development.

11.7 Angola

There must be intellectual brilliance to understand the unsustainable development in Angola despite its numerous resources. The citizens of Angola share the same fate as Nigerian citizens, and the difference is that Nigeria has been ruled by not less than 13 leaders, both military and civilian presidents, since its independence in 1960, while one man has led Angola until 2017, when a new president was elected.

After the independence from colonial Portugal, the country became a focal point in the international scuffle for power and influence between the USA, the Soviet Union, apartheid South Africa, and Cuba, each supporting various rebel groups that fuelled Angola's conflict that destroyed lives and wasted resources. Up to 1 million people were killed, and properties worth billions of dollars were damaged in the battles that lasted 27 years.

Unlike Britain and France, which surrendered their colonial posts through negotiations, Portugal resisted attempts for peaceful decolonisation. After 14 years of fighting against Portugal's colonial leadership, Angola became independent. The three significant movements fighting for the liberation of Angola were the Movement for the Liberation of Angola (MPLA), the National Front for the Liberation of Angola (FNLA), and the Union for the Total Independence of Angola, UNITA. Each of the rebel groups attracted support outside Angola. USA and DR Congo supported FNLA, the South African apartheid government supported UNITA, and MPLA was supported by the former Soviet Union and Cuba. FNLA had its stronghold in Northern Angola, while UNITA had its defence in the South. MPLA had its security in Central Angola. The country was attacked from the North by FNLA, from the South by UNITA and South Africa, and MPLA was caught in the middle.

After the defeat of Portugal's colonial government, in January 1975, the three groups signed the Alvor agreement. Because of political differences among the three groups, war broke out. In November 1975, the MPLA took charge of the capital and declared independence. After the declaration of independence by MPLA, the United Nations officially acknowledged the country as a sovereign nation, and Jose Eduardo dos Santos became the president of Angola. Within this period, the Cuban government sent up to 15,000 troops to help the MPLA repel South African forces and the UNITA rebel group from Southern Angola.

MPLA, supported by the USSR, implemented communism to rebuild the economy devastated by the war. The economic policy attracted the attention of the USA, which strives for a capitalist agenda. In 1981, apartheid South Africa attacked the Southern part of Angola to pursue SWAPO guerrilla forces active in Namibia, with their bases in Angola. The South African apartheid government's hostility in Southern Angola helped the UNITA rebels secure a territory. The aggression of South African apartheid forces and UNITA's success in the South led Cuba to respond with additional troops, thereby blocking the South African apartheid forces and UNITA advances. The fight continued until 1989, when the Angolan government, South Africa, and Cuba concluded and signed a Multilateral Agreement. The agreement resulted in UNITA under Jonas Savimbi in 1991 to stop rebel campaigns against the MPLA led government. MPLA led government initiated a series of progressive reforms; however, the USA destabilised the leftist government by maintaining an economic embargo, supporting UNITA, and withholding diplomatic recognition until after the election of 1992. MPLA, led by Dos Santos, defeated UNITA, led by Jonas Savimbi, and UNITA rejected the election results and resumed guerrilla warfare against the government.

In 1994, United Nations peacekeeping forces arrived, and a peace agreement was reached. The peace deal recommended that Savimbi become the vice president of Angola and that the UNITA rebel group be integrated into the Angola Military. The agreement was not successful but resulted in divisions and disagreements. In 1997, the UN withdrew, and Savimbi refused to participate in further negotiations. In 1998, Jonas Savimbi renewed his fight against the MPLA led government. After many attempts on his life, Jonas Savimbi was killed in a battle with Angolan government troops along riverbanks in the province of Moxico in February 2002.

Angolan leaders were played on a chess board by the USA, Cuba, and the former USSR. Dos Santos led Angola for over 38 years and handed power to his party member (Joao Lourenco), elected in 2017. During the visit of the Roman Catholic Pope (Pope Benedict XVI) to Angola in March 2009, he pleaded with Jose to remember the ever-growing poverty in his country. It is time for Angolan leaders to know they should drive for unity regardless of their differences. In agreement, they will achieve more than in tribal disunity. The development of Angola will be purely based on their commitment to creating economic diversity that will create jobs and economic growth.

11.8 Zimbabwe

Zimbabwe's crisis started in 1965 when Ian Smith, leader of Southern Rhodesia, issued a Unilateral Declaration of Independence (UDI) from Britain and imposed white-minority rule. His action prompted international sanctions and guerrilla war that claimed almost 36,000 lives and displaced nearly 1.5 million Zimbabweans by 1979. In December 1979, Britain brokered a peace deal (Lancaster House Agreement) that involved the minority government, Zimbabwe African National Union (ZANU) led by Robert Mugabe and Zimbabwe African People's Union (ZAPU) led by Joshua Nkomo. The agreement led to a ceasefire between the guerrilla groups and steps towards an independent country. It included a constitution that guaranteed majority rule and reserved 20% of parliamentary seats for the white minority. The Lancaster House Agreement led to the 1980 elections, and ZANU won with 58 of 80 seats reserved for blacks. Mugabe became Zimbabwe's PM, while Rhodesian Front won all 20 seats reserved for whites. After the election, Mugabe unleashed force on the Matabeleland, according to Crises Group.

> In the early 1980s, Mugabe unleashed brutal repression in Matabeleland and Midlands against the minority Ndebele population that supported the rival ZAPU party, dispatching North Korean-trained brigades. The five-year crackdown killed over 20,000 mainly unarmed civilians—an episode known in Zimbabwe as "Gukurahundi". ZAPU coerced 1987 into a merger with ZANU, creating ZANU-PF, paving the way for constitutional change, giving Mugabe executive presidential powers and turning the country into a de facto one-party state. Attempts to create a de jure one-party state failed in 1990, but Mugabe secured re-election in 1996.

In February 2000, ZANU-PF lost a constitutional referendum election that aimed at proposing an amendment to the constitution. The referendum's outcome led to another Zimbabwean crisis, and former war veterans began land seizures. The situation led to a chronic shortage of essential commodities and hyperinflation. In March 2000, Robert Mugabe won a presidential election, and in June of the same year, ZANU-PF defeated the Movement for Democratic Change (MDC) opposition in parliamentary elections without a two-thirds majority for the first time.

In 2005 ZANU-PF won parliamentary elections, but MDC rejected the results and alleged electoral fraud. MDC was intimidated before and after the polls, media houses that did not support the government were gagged, and human rights violations increased. In 2005, Zimbabwe was suspended by the Commonwealth of Nations supported by Nigeria, Kenya, and Australia. The UK and many Western countries sanctioned Zimbabwe. These depreciated the value of the Zimbabwe dollar and further increased the economic crisis. As the economic and social situations worsened in 2005, Zimbabwe's government launched "Operation Murambatsvina" to clear urban slums. The operation devastated the livelihoods of the slum dwellers, who were mainly poor, coupled with the dire economic situation.

In March 2007, the Mugabe-led government cracked down on the opposition. Southern Africa Development Community (SADC) mandated Thabo Mbeki, the former president of South Africa, to mediate between the ZANU-PF government and MDC. The mediation created a conducive political environment to develop a new constitution leading to free and fair elections. The mediation between the government and MDC failed, and in January 2008, Mugabe called for elections in March 2008. MDC protested and called for the election postponement until a new constitution was drafted and adopted.

On 29 March 2008, combined presidential and parliamentary elections were held. ZANU-PF lost control of the parliament to MDC, headed by Morgan Tsvangirai. The presidential election result was withheld for over a month, after which the result was released in May 2008 by the electoral officials. Tsvangirai of MDC received 47.9% of the votes, and Mugabe of ZANU-PF, 43.2%, warranted a runoff. The presidential runoff was conducted on 27 June 2008; Tsvangirai pulled out, citing election conditions that did not enhance a free and fair election. Before the runoff, the MDC leader was arrested up to four times. Mugabe won the runoff, and the outcome led to conflicts between the ruling party and MDC. Both parties agreed to hold talks, leading to a power-sharing agreement on 15 September 2008. The framework allowed Robert Mugabe to retain the position of president and Morgan Tsvangirai to become prime minister. Morgan Tsvangirai was sworn in as prime minister in February 2009.

Similarly, on 13 February 2009, a 61-member cabinet consisting of MDC and ZANU-PF members was inaugurated.

The unity government between ZANU-PF and MDC weakened the opposition. Morgan Tsvangirai was accused of corruption. The accusation of corruption and the weakness to stand firm against any government's unsustainable policies affected the outcome of Zimbabwe's elections of July 2013, which gave power to Mugabe for the fifth time since 1980. After the loss of the election by the MDC in 2013, some of the leaders of the MDC called for a leadership change and the resignation of Morgan Tsvangirai, but he snubbed the resignation request. The refusal of Morgan Tsvangirai highlighted the problem of leadership in opposition parties in Africa, where most political parties' internal democracies are not effective.

The continuous misusing of power by Robert Mugabe, the constant interference in administration by his wife, Grace Mugabe, and the removal of the Zimbabwe vice president in November 2017 led to a military coup lasting more than two weeks. The coup led to Robert Mugabe's resignation as Zimbabwe's president, and Emmerson Mnangagwa, the removed former vice president, was brought back from exile in South Africa to become Zimbabwean president. He appointed a new cabinet and pledged to improve Zimbabwe's economy. His first step to economic recovery was to cancel the indigenisation policy of businesses in Zimbabwe except for mining.

In July 2018, the Zimbabwe government conducted an election. Emmerson Mnangagwa contested under Zanu-PF, and Nelson Chamisa was the MDC presidential aspirant. Zanu-PF won the parliamentary majority with 144 seats. MDC won 64 seats, an improvement from the 44 seats the party won in 2013. The presidential election was won by Emmerson Mnangagwa by 50.8% of votes against Nelson Chamisa by 44.3%, and independent presidential candidates pulled 5% in all.

The crisis in Zimbabwe was exacerbated by the consequences of Robert Mugabe's intolerance, poor economic strategy, and oppression of the opposition, which led to development challenges. The weak and unresponsive opposition led by Morgan Tsvangirai was not practical, and it was divisive. The internal politics of the opposition MDC did not help shape a better country for the Zimbabweans, partly because of the dictatorial tendencies of Mugabe and the weak leadership of Morgan Tsvangirai. The crisis is also bullying by the former colonial UK. Mukori (2015) said it is vital to recognise that Zimbabwe was not always like this and did not have to be like this. He asserted that Robert Mugabe's tyranny was not an accident and Britain played a shameful part in Zimbabwe's economic woes. Johnson further stated that it was the betrayal of the Lancaster House agreement that gave Mugabe his pretext to launch his "pogroms" against the whites, which resulted in Zimbabwe's economic crunch because the economy of Zimbabweans is in the hands of the minority whites. The Boris Johnson statements were correct. As said earlier in the book, the West should not be exonerated from Africa's challenges. The argument still maintains that the major challenge is weak leadership.

Many people believe Mugabe's policy on land redistribution is the root of the crisis. Land redistribution was needed, but the policy, strategy, and implementation required were more questionable. The poor execution of the policy could be linked to the arrogant behaviours of some members of the minority white and the bullying tactics by the Zanu-PF. The land redistribution lacked transparency and was shredded by nepotism and favouritism, which did not favour Zimbabwe's poor. Furthermore, the lack of commitment by Britain to keep faith with the Lancaster agreement to pay white farmers to release some land to black Zimbabweans was the igniter of the land crises in Zimbabwe.

Zimbabwe used to be known for its exportation of food and as one of the industrial powers of Africa; since the collapse of the economy and the existence of many investors, the country has relied heavily on food aid and the importation of goods and services. The government of Zimbabwe blamed external factors for the economic challenges. As pointed out earlier, the economic difficulties are the action of Zimbabwe's weak leadership and Western interference and arrogance.

CHAPTER 12

Conclusion

12.1 Summary

Pre-colonial Africa was developing politically, socially, and economically; there were social and economic institutions managing the affairs of the communities and developing regulations and laws, even though most of them were orally transmitted. Africa was evolving and had universities and astronomies before the white men came. They have developed iron, cloth dying, and irrigation and have architectural styles. They have developed political systems and democratic structures. They have calendars such as the Igbo and Ethiopian calendar. This shows the rate in Africa was set before the white men came. What happened during colonial and post colonial Africa when the white men left is a concern?

Presently, more houses are built in Africa, more people are driving cars, there is better access to communication systems and more schools have been constructed and possibly more health centres. Understandably, more people can access roads, IT infrastructure, water, electricity, and other related infrastructural developments. However, human development capacity in many African countries is shallow compared to the 1960s and 1970s. There is more deindustrialisation, higher level of multidimensional poverty, more health crises, more increase in school dropouts, more corruption and frauds, gender challenges have increased, older people still hold on to power while the youths are pushed to the periphery of

C. E. Osuigwe, *Leadership and Economic Development Challenges in Post-Colonial Africa*, Sustainable Development Goals Series,
https://doi.org/10.1007/978-3-031-45663-3_12

governance in many countries; girls' child is still given out in marriage earlier. The challenges are getting more and more than in the 1960s to 1980s. Today, we have greater/better access to hospitals, but there are more health crises while the ratios of doctors to population are decreasing. As the population increases, fewer and fewer people have access to infrastructure and service delivery.

The population increase has increased demand for goods and services with little production in Africa. It has led to Africans yielding more to foreign importation of goods and services. More importation of goods shows a low level of entrepreneurship and innovation of African indigenous industries for industrial growth. It highlights the limitations in transforming Africa's abundant natural resources to finish goods. The limit is because of inadequate infrastructural development.

The major challenge in the continent is pseudo-leaders. These leaders have kept Africa down through dictatorship, abuse of power, and change of the constitution to remain in power. These leaders have assumed cultic figures that followers can kill at will. These pseudo-leaders encourage the rigging of elections and disenfranchise the continent's citizens. They rely on intimidation and harassment of the opposition. They hate transparency and accountability. They are the principal architects of Africa's challenges.

The African problem has assumed the nature of a chameleon that keeps changing colours depending on who is in power. The issues remain in different dimensions because of greed, ethnicity, nepotism, and favouritism that fuel corruption and fraud. These problems are dynamic because many leaders and political elites are very divisive in their leadership to suit their selfish agenda. The exploitative leadership enhances the unfair judicial system, mismanagement, ethnic politics, and sentiments in delivering good governance. The mechanism for exploitative and destructive leadership is state capture, which has become a norm since early 2000. It has been in Nigeria for over three decades and surfaced in South Africa.

For the past two decades, the continent has seen deindustrialisation and dwindling agricultural production compared to population growth. Similarly, the youth bulge in Asia led to the rapid development of Asia after colonisation and Asian countries tapped into the youths' energy and developed their countries. In Africa, youths and women are consigned to the periphery of economic decision-making, where their voices cannot be heard, and they cannot make valuable suggestions for social and economic development.

The leadership has weakened education through a lack of budget to develop the standard education system in some African countries. Some policies and strategies could be more robust, corruption is impeding better education, and the continent's children have less access to schools. Corruption in education is reducing the development of infrastructure and the quality of education. Similarly, the skills needed for Africa are migrating daily, leaving the continent vulnerable to economic challenges. The migration is noticeable among professionals and the health sector.

Gender issues keep lingering, and women bear significant societal and economic challenges. They care for the family and the children's upbringing and are more domesticated than men. Hence, any economic problems and difficulties affect women and children the most. Conflicts in Africa affect women and female children more than male children and men. Male children stand greater chances to go to school than female children; men are more likely to have leadership roles entrusted to them in Africa than women. Men have more chances of getting a job or economic opportunities than women. Sustainable economic growth in Africa will be challenging until women are encouraged to participate in social and economic development.

The social and economic problems in Africa led to thousands and thousands of deaths of many Africans in the Mediterranean Sea trying to cross Europe for a better life. Economic challenges led to many tribal conflicts, Afrophobia, and xenophobia attacks in Africa, which are signs of weak, visionless, and clueless leaders. More challenges are witnessed in consistent conflicts that endanger Africa's integration and investments, increase capital flight, damage to infrastructure, school dropouts, ethnic crisis, and lingering economic problems.

Ethnic politics have bedevilled many countries like Nigeria, Uganda, and Kenya. Ivory Coast's policy of "Ivorite" initiated conflicts in a stable government. The religious disputes engineered in Sudan devastated the country for years, killing millions. The ethnic patronage and greed for diamonds and gold destroyed DRC Congo. Zimbabwe's non-strategic land redistribution and the arrogance of the white minority destabilised one of the economic hubs of Africa. The challenges are enormous and need leaders with good intentions and integrity to direct the continent in the right direction. Some of the suggestions for policy and strategic development are mentioned below.

12.2 Recommendation

Nkrumanh (1961) states Africa needs dedicated, informed, and honest citizens. Paul Kagame said, "I would rather argue that we need to mobilise the right mindsets rather than funding. After all, in Africa, we have everything we need in real terms. Whatever we are lacking, we have the means to acquire, and yet, we remain mentally married to the idea that nothing can get moving without external finance. We are even begging for things we already have, which is a mindset failure". The fact is that Africa needs people with the right mindset and integrity. Africa needs leaders who will submerge themselves in national building and development. Leaders whose humility is their strength and integrity is not questionable. Africa's memories during the colonial and the present leaders make a sad story, but for how long? Africa must find a solution in unity of purpose and vision, not greed. Africa has the resources and skills at home and in the diaspora, and youths who share dreams of greatness should promote the following.

1. Africa should build their communities by contributing in the following ways.
    a. Transform the communities through volunteering for community services promoting awareness for gender emancipation and youths' empowerment.
    b. Show compassion, understand people's plights, identify goodness in others, and use them instead of searching out their faults.
    c. Identify progressive ideas in your communities and build on them. This will assist in making the community for common national goals and visions.
    d. A recognisable system should award merit great achievers in African countries. Such awards should be extended to ordinary people like market women, rural men and women, and individuals who have contributed to their community's development and empowerment. The award should not be based only on financial or intellectual contributions; merit recognition should be above party, ethnic, and racial considerations. Those who achieve merits should be brought to leadership in Africa. In doing this, Africa will build a community of encouragement, empowerment, self-resilience, and upliftment.

2. Financial aid is not the solution to Africa's development. African countries that receive financial aid should start working hard to grow their economy and have less reliance on financial aid. However, financial aid donors should look towards development opportunities in Africa and act on them if they genuinely want Africa to develop sustainably. This will assist in community development rather than economic dependence. Depending on financial aid from the Western world is like an adult who has formed the habit of receiving food from his parents and finds it hard to go out to look for a job or try a simple roadside business to make a living. Countries that depend on financial aid might need help to move to a self-sustaining economy. Rwanda is an excellent example of an aid recipient for budgets and relies on countries' investments for its allocations. There are few natural resources in Denmark, Belgium, Israel, and many other developed countries. Still, they are economic powerhouses. For example, Israel transformed most of their un-arable desert into fertile, productive agricultural land. Most African countries, including low-income people, have good agricultural land. African countries need good agricultural sector plans and strategies and the implementation of such plans to be transparent and accountable. It will lead to food production and security for the nations and enhance human development security. Therefore, there is a need for research on the high production of crops and animals, more irrigation, and access to agricultural facilities, and improve market access for farmers. African farmers also need better weather and climate forecasts and information technology by giving them access to the internet and IT technologies. There is a need to investigate land tenure to ensure the security of land for rural farmers and small-scale farmers. Accessibility to finance should be encouraged with low rates for repayment of loans. Also, repayment of loans should be spread for a more extended period of not less than 20 years to allow the creation of jobs and food sustainability. The government should do more towards providing grants to rural farmers and other support services such as forming and managing large cooperative groups.
3. African countries should focus on developing policies and strategies for skill development based on indigenous knowledge, apprenticeship schemes, and vocational education. A good economy is created by vibrant policies and strategies that empower citizens. The policies and

strategies should encourage entrepreneurship, the creation of jobs, and massive production through agriculture and SMMEs.

4. Solving the continent's political, social, and economic challenges lies with no group. There is no race, tribe, community, group, intellectual, wealthy, middle class, poor, or interest group that can claim monopoly to wisdom, innovation, and intelligence. Therefore, the solution lies with all Africans. There is a problem when a particular group is considered the solution to a problem and challenge because the wisdom to provide solutions might lie outside the selected group, tribe, community, intellectual, or interest group. Therefore, answers to Africa's problems lie overwhelmingly in the participation of all, particularly with due respect to all minority ethnic groups, because wisdom is not the property of any majority group. Emeka Odumegwu Ojukwu (1989), in his book *Because I Am Involved*, advised the Nigerian leadership to continue to check economic and social imbalances, remembering that no condition is permanent. He further stated that those disfavoured for one reason or another in 1960 were not necessarily disfavoured in those exact domains in 1989. In the passage of time and the effort to balance, others might have become disfavoured. By checking social and economic imbalances and mitigating them, the inequalities are reduced, and job creation is enhanced.
5. The continent should revolutionise the social and political system. The old political elites should accommodate a fresh mindset and allow the active participation of the youth. The revolution should involve the aggressive involvement of youths in political parties, where candidates are nominated for political positions. Youths should seize the opportunities in political parties and select right-thinking and hard-working youths for representation. The youths should be involved in civil society through which their grievances can be shown and channelled. The youth's voice should be responsible for guarding democracy, transparency, and accountable governance.
6. African women have proved that they have the potential for sustainable African development. In countries where women participate in social, political, and economic decisions, the results are outstanding; an example is Rwanda. Many exceptional African women can become great presidents in Africa. African women are intellectually and skillfully prepared to be allowed up to 50% leadership positions. Women grasp household issues better, which are the main concern for family and society development. Poverty and unemployment affect women.

Thus, it is essential to know that involving women strategically in leadership will go a long way in solving Africa's problems. They understand the rudiments of society more than their male counterparts because of their closeness to the environment and families. They have shown many times that they are result-oriented. Equally, women's education should be encouraged, and policies and strategies should be implemented to promote girls' education and political participation. Women's inclusion in leadership is not to be a subject of debate; it is a necessity of the time.

7. For Africa to succeed, there must be recognition and respect for professionalism while assisting one another in their career development. However, respect in workplaces is earned; it is not a title. Respect for professionalism will go a long way in solving African development problems and enhancing the confidence needed for quality, efficiency, and effectiveness. Africans should continue to strive to carry out their functions and duties professionally in organisations, institutions, and businesses. The major obstacle to achieving professionalism in Africa is greed and hunger to get rich quickly without working for it. Therefore, professionalism should be the first consideration before any other thing in a place of work or duty. Gradually, it will become a culture in serving clients.

All Africans, in particular academics, leaders, and political elites, should not be emotional regarding the ill-discipline in the development of African society. For corruption to be minimised to a greater extent, people must be held accountable for their deeds. Personal emotion should be set aside when a brother, a child, a colleague, a relation, or a friend is implicated in corrupt activities. They should face the consequences of violating the law rather than state institutions being used to protect unscrupulous individuals because of political alliance, family relationships, or friendship. Business in Africa must be carried out with ethical principles of great values and morality. These would help to drive sustainable African development. If Africans do not do away with emotions regarding corrupt people, Africa's development challenges will not be easy to overcome. An African leader linked to unethical behaviour should be prosecuted. There have been cases where leaders were caught in corrupt activities, but instead of hauling them to court to be charged, they were asked to resign. It does not encourage the fight against corruption. There should be no resignation of a corrupt leader without prosecution in the court. To avoid engendering professional and ethical behaviours promoting social and economic development sustainability, all unscrupulous individuals must be prosecuted. Because of high levels of corruption in Africa, immunity clauses that protect presidents, prime ministers, governors, and premiers from prosecution while in office should be removed from the constitutions. This will go a long way to reducing corruption and unethical behaviours.

Anti-corruption organisations and institutions should be separated from the executive arms of governments. Civil societies should be a party to selecting the heads of institutions and organisations fighting corruption and fraud. The heads of anti-corruption organisations should not be a politician but a professional in investigation and laws. This is to avoid interference from the government leaders and political elites. Civil organisations and judiciary institutions should be engaged when appointing anti-corruption institutional leadership. Civil organisations and judiciary institutions should be allowed to monitor the activities of such anti-corruption institutions. This process will reduce executive interference in the anti-corruption fight. All the anti-corruption institutions in Africa should collaborate and share information to fight corruption in Africa.

8. African countries should develop a keen research interest and be at the forefront of research on the continent. Research should be on every aspect of human and society development that will enhance policy and strategic development and encourage technological innovation and industrial development. The study must necessitate transparent and accountable leadership to reap its benefits. To promote research, government institutions and private organisations should provide a budget. The government should use research results to develop policies, strategies, and products to enhance sustainable social and economic development. All the PhD research must be linked to projects, programmes, production and policy or strategic developments.
9. Because of the endemic corruption and constant conflict in the continent, there is a need for individual audits and declarations of interest and assets. People with questionable characters and dealings should not be allowed to vie for political positions or allowed to take up executive positions in the government or institutions. When people with suspicious characters are allowed to participate in leadership

positions, it sends a wrong message to the people. Thus, stopping such questionable characters will encourage people with ideas and ethics to participate in governance and their social and economic development. Individual audits in Africa will assist in alleviating corruption and minimising conflicts.

10. The issues of Ubuntu and Nwanne should be integral to mobilisation and awareness. Individuals' greed and selfishness could be overcome by embracing the philosophies of Nwanne and Ubuntu. Acquiring wealth should not be to oppress the disadvantaged in society or to show off but rather a way of assisting the communities and building a sustainable society. People appointed to high positions and businesses awarded contracts by the government should be able to demonstrate how many communities or individuals they have assisted in boosting their social and economic status through corporate social responsibilities. Great African achievers in every sphere of life should mentor upcoming ones so that there should be sustainable development. This is in the spirit of Nwanne and Ubuntu. In the spirit of Nwanne and Ubuntu, there should be capacity development through motivation and encouragement by engaging educated Africans in the diaspora to contribute to African development. It should be backed by the determination of leaders and political elites not to interfere in professional responsibilities and create a thriving environment for social and economic development, an environment devoid of leaders' and political elites' meddling in strategic issues in pursuit of selfish agendas.
11. Employment must not be based on party alliance, ethnicity, and favouritism but on experience and expertise. The government should develop empowerment programmes for graduates so they can easily be assimilated into the growing economy. Employment in Africa should neglect where one comes from, which ethnic group one belongs to, or the political party one belongs to rather than the qualifications and expertise needed for a job. Proper skills and ethics create employment and enhance sustainable social and economic development. When the right person is employed, more jobs are created, and people lose jobs when the wrong person is employed.
12. The innovation of African cultures and traditions should be significant in pursuing sustainable development in Africa, particularly in branding and marketing African food, spices, music, African attires, beer, gin, wine, and other African products. Leaders and political elites should support indigenous products. Government institutions

and organisations should encourage industries that manufacture 100% made in Africa by procuring their products. These will create jobs, enhance domestic investment, and attract foreign investment into local initiatives.

13. African problems are linked to the inability to use African indigenous languages to communicate in the local economy. This problem is compounded by poor drive and energy to promote African languages through media, research, and entertainment. African language should be of paramount importance to the development of Africa. It will enhance the local population's understanding of development strategies and encourage the incorporation of traditional and cultural ideas into development policies. The use of African languages will integrate communities for local economic development. Africa's diverse languages are blessings and assets. This is because language diversity creates unique cultures and values, thereby bequeathing distinctive identities to individuals and reducing isolation and homogenisation. Linguistic diversity is like biodiversity. Each language in a society reflects a unique worldview and cultural complex, mirroring the routine in which a speech community has resolved its problems in dealing with the world and has expressed its thinking, classification of philosophy, and understanding of the world around it.

    Ethnic groups in Africa should take a good look at the ways the Jews embraced their lifestyle. In almost all the major cities in the world, there are Jewish schools that teach young Jews about their history, culture, tradition, and language. This drive sustains the growth of the Jewish image and their beliefs and preserves their culture, tradition, and language. But in Africa, it is a different story. Some languages are fading away, while some leaders and political elites act uninformed of the ill, affecting society. For Africa to develop, indigenous languages should be used to communicate in social and economic development. This enhances the development of local content. Therefore, there is a need to develop language policies to strengthen the use of indigenous African languages for national development. All the books used in primary, secondary, and university can be translated into indigenous languages. It does not stop the use of English, French, or Spanish in areas with multiethnic integration.

14. Freedom of speech should be embraced at all costs. No matter how an argument sounds, African leaders and political elites (who tend to suppress minority and opposition voices) should not stop opposition

voices. Any form of constitutional provision that inhibits people from expressing their personal opinions should be removed because it hinders sustainable democracy, governance, and development. Debates and arguments are not attacks but about differences in personal and political ideals. Leadership should desist from the blame game but critically criticise leadership challenges. Criticism should be seen as a contribution to the development of a country, and positive criticism helps shape policy and strategic development.

15. In most cases in Africa, resolving conflicts involves rebel groups' leaders without involving the aggrieved communities. Fixing a problem with one person or group of people (Rebel Leaders) does not mean that the problem has been solved as far as the people or communities are still feeling aggrieved. Rebel leaders do not always represent the feelings and wishes of the aggrieved communities. Rebel leaders often capitalise on communities' grievances and use their emotions to cause conflicts. When a rebel leader accepts the conditions for resolving a conflict based on selfish motives and greed, those conditions might not be in the interest of the aggrieved community or communities. There is a certainty that the conflicts are bound to restart in the future with another rebel leader emerging to lead the distressed communities. Therefore, resolving conflicts should involve the community representatives and all the stakeholders in the community.
16. Similarly, disarmed rebels should be positively absorbed and integrated into society to avoid future conflicts. Leadership should be able to monitor any future occurrence of conflicts. Monitoring conflicts involves understanding the challenges the communities go through, the crisis communities face, and the grievances that arise in mining areas and land distributions and mitigating the causes of their grievances.
17. Some of the remunerations to parliamentarians can be used for infrastructure development. Nigerian senator overall earns at least eight times as much as American senator and as much as three times the American president. Egbosiuba (2011) states, "Nigerian senator takes home at least $1.40 million which comprises $1.28m quarterly allocation, $0.113m regular salaries and allowances compared to about $0. 174m (₦21million) American senator and members of the House of Representatives takes home. United Kingdom's parliament member earns about £64,766 (N15m). This means that Nigerian federal legislatures are paid more than twice what British member of parliament

makes per annum. Further check reveals that the Nigerian senate president takes home about ₦250m quarterly or ₦83.33m monthly. Senate deputy president gets ₦150m per quarter or ₦50m a month, earning in 4 months, six times what the British prime minister earns in a year. The British prime minister David Cameron makes about £190,000 per annum (₦44m) while the United States president earns $400,000 annually". Nigeria spends almost 25% of its budget on the National Assembly; this is terrific. It is frightening in the face of infrastructural problems in Nigeria; it is scary to note the poor educational and health facilities. This money can solve most of Nigeria's infrastructure challenges if adequately utilised. In view of this, African countries should start looking at part-time parliamentarians and lawmakers with their own jobs and should be paid on the days and hours they are involved in legislative activities. Also, countries with two legislative chambers should discard one to minimise governance costs and improve infrastructural development.

12.3 Closing Remarks

Bemba Tribe Proverb in Zambia: "Amafi banyela ukutali" (He who wants to defecate should go far into the bush; if not, the smell will come and hunt him),

Igbo Tribe Proverb: "A fowl that gloated over the butchering of a fellow fowl knew not that the fate that befell the fellow fowl would soon befall it".

Igbo Proverb: "You will not die if you did not work hard but will live to regret why you did not work hard".

Krio Proverb from Sierra Leone: "If you throw ashes, ashes will follow you".

Igbo Proverb: "He who went to the bush to fetch ants' infected wood invited lizards to his house".

Nigerian Proverb: "Do not throw stones in a marketplace because, if it did not fall on your child or relation, it might fall on your neighbour".

Swahili Proverb: "Do not abuse midwives while children are still being born".

Cameroon Proverb: "He who does not look ahead always remains behind".

Sepedi Proverb: "Lions that do not work together can be defeated by a limping buffalo".

Martin Luther Jr.: "If a man is called to be a street sweeper, he should sweep streets even as Michelangelo painted, or Beethoven composed music, or Shakespeare wrote poetry. He should sweep streets so well that all the hosts of heaven and earth will pause to say, here lived a great street sweeper who did his job well".

African Proverb: "If you want to go fast, go alone, but if you want to go far, go together".

References

Abbas J. (2018); Women grow 70% of Africa's food. But have few rights over the land they tend. https://www.weforum.org/agenda/2018/03/women-farmers-food-production-land-rights/. Accessed 25 February 2020.

Achebe C., (2012); "There was a County", The Penguin Press New York.

Achebe C., (1984); "The Trouble with Nigeria", Heinemann Publishers Ltd, Oxford.

Achebe C., (1958); "Things Fall Apart". William Heinemann Ltd.

AFDB (2013; An Integrated Approach to Infrastructure Provision in Africa. African Development Bank. https://www.afdb.org/fileadmin/uploads/afdb/Documents/Publications/Economic_Brief_-_An_Integrated_Approach_to_Infrastructure_Provision_in_Africa.pdf. Accessed July 2020.

AFDB (2018); Africa's Infrastructure: Great Potential but Little Impact on Inclusive Growth. https://www.afdb.org/fileadmin/uploads/afdb/Documents/Publications/2018AEO/African_Economic_Outlook_2018_-_EN Chapter3.pdf. Accessed 22 May 2019.

Africanus L., (1550); Geographical History of Africa https://onlinebooks.library.upenn.edu/webbin/book/lookupid?key=olbp7677. Accessed June 2020.

Aheisibwe A R., Karoubi E M., Dushime O., Fuller G., Twinoburyo E. N , and Abigail Simkoko A., (2020); Africa SDG Index and Dashboards Report 2020. Pica Publishing Ltd, South Africa.

Annan K., (2003); New Instrument Described as New Framework for Action against 'Insidious Plague. https://press.un.org/en/2003/sgsm8977.doc.htm. Accessed July 10, 2020.

C. E. Osuigwe, *Leadership and Economic Development Challenges in Post-Colonial Africa*, Sustainable Development Goals Series,
https://doi.org/10.1007/978-3-031-45663-3

Anti-Slavery Commissioner, (2016); The Global Salary Index 2016. The Minderoo Foundation Pty Ltd. All rights reserved. Printed in Australia/United Kingdom/ India.

Barker A., (2017), Theresa May's Florence Speech Annotated. Financial Times, https://ig.ft.com/theresa-may-florence-speech-annotated/. Accessed 13 May 2020.

Barry M., (2015); Sailing to Utopia: Oscar Wilde on Altruism and Anarchism, Irish Philosophy. https://www.irishphilosophy.com/2015/10/15/utopia-wilde/#:~:text=The%20article%20quotes%20Oscar%20Wilde,discontented%2C%20disobedient%2C%20and%20rebellious. Accessed 10 March 2019.

Beegle K., Christiaensen L., Dabalen A., & Gaddies I. S., (2016); A World Bank Group report titled African Poverty Report. 2016 International Bank for Reconstruction and Development / The World Bank 1818 H Street NW, Washington DC 20433.

Bennett N., (2001); "Corruption in Education System in Developing Countries: What it is doing to the Young: 10th International-anti Corruption Conference that took place in Prague, Czech Republic, From 7–11 October 2001.

Bhargara A., Docquier F., & Moullan Y., (2011); Modeling the Effects of Physician Emigration on Human Development. https://doi.org/10.1016/j.ehb.2010.12.004. Source PubMed, accessed 22 January 2021

Bold T., Filmer D., Martin G., Molina E., Stacy B., Rockmore C., Svensson J., & Wane W., (2017). Enrolment without Learning: Teacher Effort, Knowledge, and Skill in Primary Schools in Africa. Journal of Economic Perspectives—Volume 31, Number 4—Fall 2017—Pages 185–204.

Boko S., (2018); Illicit financial flows continue to impede Africa's development. https://archive.uneca.org/stories/illicit-financial-flows-continue-impede-africa%E2%80%99s-development-says-eca%E2%80%99s-boko-hlpd-2018. Accessed 28 July 2022.

Chirikure S., (2018) "Precolonial Metallurgy and Mining across Africa" https://oxfordre.com/africanhistory/view/10.1093/acrefore/9780190277734.001.0001/acrefore-9780190277734-e-148. Oxford Research Encyclopaedia. Accessed 30 May 2019.

CNBC (2016); Africa spends $1bn yearly on medical tourism abroad – WB. https://www.cnbcafrica.com/media/5607097873001/. Accessed May 2022.

Costa A. M., (2007); Anti-Corruption Climate Change: it started in Nigeria 6th National Seminar on Economic Crime Abuja, 13 November 2007. https://www.unodc.org/unodc/en/about-unodc/speeches/2007-11-13.html. Accessed 10 June 2013.

Dakolias M., (2003); "The Role of the judiciary for economic and Social Development: Speech to the EU Judiciary Representative, The Hague, Netherlands.

Egbosiuba M., (2011); Jumbo Pay of Nigerian Legislatures. https://www.allthingsnigeria.com/2011/jumbo-pay-of-nigerian-legislatures/. Accessed 27 July 2023.

FAO (2018); Africa Regional Overview of Food Security and Nutrition. https://www.fao.org/3/ca2710en/CA2710EN.pdf, Accessed 23 April 2021.

GF (2019); Poorest Countries in the World: https://www.gfmag.com/global-data/economic-data/the-poorest-countries-in-the-world: Accessed 20 May 2019.

Global Coalition for Africa (2004); African Social and Economic Trends, 2003/2004, Washington, DC.

Gouredou E., (2023); Without massive investment, drinking water will remain a scarce resource for Africa. https://blogs.worldbank.org/youth-transforming-africa/without-massive-investment-drinking-water-will-remain-scarce-resource. Accessed 05 July 2023.

Guest R., (2004); "The Shackled Continent" Power, Corruption, and Africa Lives. Smithsonian Books in Association with Macmillian.

Hamann K., (2003); Corruption, a Critical Obstacle for Social Développent. https://2001-2009.state.gov/p/inl/rls/rm/31027.htm. Accessed 20 May 2021

Hansson S. O., (2003); "Decision Theory" Department of Philosophy and History of Technology: Royal Institute of Technology, Stockholm.

Harris L., (2006); "Truth – Telling"; Confronting the reality of the lack of Candor inside Organization posted on this website www.linkageinc.com Accessed 15 October 2011.

IANSA, OXFAM & Saferworld (2007); "Africa's Missing Billions; International Arms flow and the Cost of Conflict. https://oxfamilibrary.openrepository.com/bitstream/handle/10546/123908/bp-africas-missing-billions-111007-en.pdf;jsessionid=D08962D4296BD0F39F66F59A1580CEA1?sequence=1. Accessed 12 February 2016.

Ilibagiza I., (2006); Left to Tell. Hay House; Later Printing edition.

Justice Initiative (2010); Corruption and its Consequences in Equatorial Guinea: A brief paper by Open Society. https://www.justiceinitiative.org/uploads/d40113c2-7e4a-41f6-8dec-5b9846d00546/equatorial-guinea-20100317.pdf. Accessed 29 August 2012.

ILO (2003); Wounded Childhood: The Use of Children in Armed Conflict in Central Africa. ILO Publications, International Labour Office, CH-1211 Geneva 22, Switzerland.

Igwe U., (2012a); "The Many Faces of Kenyan Politics" http://africanheraldexpress.com/blog7/2012/02/15/the-many-faces-of-kenyan politics/.

Igwe U., (2012b); "Obiang and the kleptocrats in Africa" http://www.punchng.com/opinion/obiang-and-the-kleptocrats-in-africa/ 14/03/2012.

Kharas H., Hamel K., and Hofer M., (2018); "The Start of New Poverty Narrative a report" https://www.brookings.edu/blog/future-development/2018/06/19/the-start-of-a-new-poverty-narrative/ (19/06/2018).

Klein N (2007); The Shock Doctrine; The Rise of Disaster Capitalism. Metropolitan Books.

Koutoni M., (2016); Story of Cities: Benin City, Mighty Medieval Capital now lost without Trace. https://www.theguardian.com/cities/2016/mar/18/story-of-cities-5-benin-city-edo-nigeria-mighty-medieval-capital-lost-without-trace. Accessed 15 November 2019.

Machobane, L.B.B.J., (1990); Government and Change in Lesotho, 1800–1966: A study of political institutions. New York: St. Martins Press.

Mandela, N., (1995); Long Walk to Freedom (Macdonald Purnel, London).

May J., (2000) "Poverty and Inequality in South Africa" David Philip Publishers (Pty) Ltd. 208 Werdmuller Centre, 7708 South Africa.

Mbalela Z., (2012); Pikoli lambasts political leaders. https://www.sowetanlive.co.za/news/2012-07-05-pikoli-lambasts-political-leaders/. Accessed 10 July 2020.

Mbeki M., (2009); "Architects of Poverty" – Why African Capitalist Needs Changing; Picador Africa.

Mbeki M. (ed) (2011); "Advocate for Change"; How to Overcome Africa's Challenges; Picador Africa, Johannesburg.

Mohamoud A.A., (2005); "Reversing the Brain Drain in Africa". Harnessing the Intellectual Capital of the Diaspora for Knowledge Development in Africa. Feasibility Study to SAHAN by Netherland Organization for International Cooperation in Higher Education (NUFFC).

Mitchel J., (2019); African e-Connectivity Index 2021: The final frontier and a huge opportunity. https://www.investmentmonitor.ai/tech/africa-connectivity-index-2021/. Accessed 11 March 2021.

Mitchel J., (2021); African e-Connectivity Index 2021: The final frontier and a huge opportunity. https://www.investmentmonitor.ai/tech/africa-connectivity-index-2021/. Accessed 11 March 2021.

Mohamed H. & Chughtai A., (2019); What you need to know about Africa Refugees. https://www.aljazeera.com/news/2019/2/9/what-you-need-to-know-about-africas-refugees. Accessed 21 February 2023.

Mukori W., (2015); London Mayor Boris Johnson Boosts Mugabe. https://www.zimeye.net/2015/02/25/londonmayor-boris-johnson-boosts-mugabe-2/. Accessed 21 February 2022.

Ncana N., (2010); 20 Years to Break Schools Backlog. Times Live, https://www.timeslive.co.za/news/south-africa/2010-03-23-20-years-to-break-schools-backlog/. Accessed 2 June 2020.

Nkrumanh K., (1961); I Speak of Freedom; a Statement of African Ideology. Mercury Books No. 37.

Nkrumah, K., (1965); Neo-Colonialism, The Last Stage of imperialism. London: Thomas Nelson & Sons, Ltd.

Obama B., (2013); Remarks by the President on College Affordability – Buffalo, NY. Office of the Press Secretary. State University of New York Buffalo Buffalo, New York.

Ojoye T., (2018); Eight politicians with N232bn corruption cases working for Buhari's re-election. https://punchng.com/eight-politicians-with-n232bn-corruption-cases-working-for-buharis-re-election/. Accessed 14 July 2023.

Ojukwu O., E., (1989); Because I was Involved. Publisher: Spectrum Books Ltd., Ibadan, 1989.

Plaizier W., (2016); "2 Truths about Africa's Agriculture" https://www.weforum.org/agenda/2016/01/how-africa-can-feed-the-world/.

Schaltuper A., (2018); Two-thirds of Africa Population still do not have Access to Electricity – and its is Threatening the Security of the Continent. https://www.independent.co.uk/voices/africa-energy-poverty-afdb-kenya-nigeria-lpg-gdp-electricity-europe-global-south-a8449626.html. Accessed 30 November 2022.

Selassie's H., (1963); Towards African Unity. The Journal of Modern African Studies Vol. 1, No. 3 (Sep., 1963), pp. 281–291. Published By: Cambridge University Press.

Rescher, N., (1988); Rationality: A Philosophical Inquiry into The Nature and the Rationale of Reason, Clarendon Press, Oxford.

Osuigwe C., (2011); *Shopping Leakage*: Case Study of Maseru, VDM Verleg Dr. Muller Gmbh & Co. KG. Germany.

Naidoo P., (2023); South Africa's Economic Contraction Exceeds All Estimates. https://www.bloomberg.com/news/articles/2023-03-07/south-african-economy-contracts-on-intensifying-power-outages#:~:text=The%20electricity%20crisis%20is%20costing,Treasury's%20growth%20estimate%20of%20 0.9%25. Accessed 3 July 2023.

Niekerk J., (2013); "UBUNTU AND MORAL VALUE" A thesis submitted to the Faculty of Humanities, University of the Witwatersrand, Johannesburg, in fulfilment of the requirements for the degree of Doctor of Philosophy.

Nuruddeen M. A., (2010); Inside Ghana's Collapsing Textile Industry. http://inwent-iij-lab.org Accessed 29 June 2010.

Ratcliffe S., (2018); Oxfords Essential Quotations (3 ed). Oxford University Press.

Ratcliffe S., (2016); Oxfords Essential Quotations (4 ed). Oxford University Press.

Rodney W., (1973); "How Europe Underdeveloped Africa" Bogle-L Ouverture Publication, London and Tanzanian Publishing House, Dar-Es-Salaam, Transcript from 6th reprint, 1973.

Sherwood C., (2020); Black History Month 2020. Benin Court Art 11. https://wmag.culturewarrington.org/2020/10/14/black-history-month-2020 benin-court-art-ii/. Accessed January 2022.

Transference International (2012–2017); Corruption Index. https://www.transparency.org/en/cpi/2021?gclid=Cj0KCQjwho-lBhC_ARIsAMpgMocykH8c2oBGLjfigLHEy_4yuZmKQI1V3Lwh2q4JYkhu54hlhIUXEBcaAj66EALw_wcB. Accessed 20 May 2019.

UN (2019); UN World Water Development Report 2019: 'Leaving no one behind'. https://www.unwater.org/news/un-world-water-development-report-2019-%E2%80%98leaving-no-one-behind%E2%80%99. Accessed 20 March 2021.

UN (2025); United Nations: The Millennium Development Goals Report 2015 Embargoed until 6 July, 10:15 am EDT (GMT-4)). https://www.un.org/millenniumgoals/2015_MDG_Report/pdf/MDG%202015%20PR%20Key%20Facts%20Regional.pdf. Accessed 15 August 2020.

UN (2001); Security Council Condemns Illegal Exploitation of Democratic Republic of Congo's Natural Resources. https://press.un.org/en/2001/sc7057.doc.htm#:~:text=The%20Security%20Council%20this%20afternoon,the%20conflict%20in%20that%20country. Accessed March 2012.

UNDP (2005); Human Development Report: International Cooperation at a Crossroads: Aid Trade and Security in an Unequal World, New York. https://hdr.undp.org/content/human-development-report-2005. Accessed 16 July 2011.

UNHCR (----); Current Emergencies. https://www.unhcr.org/about-unhcr/where-we-work/africa. Accessed 04 July 2023.

UNICEF (---); Comparison for Literacy and Primary School Enrolment https://data.unicef.org/topic/education/overview/.

UNICEF (2020); Africa to drastically accelerate progress on water, sanitation, and hygiene – report. https://www.unicef.org/senegal/en/press-releases/africa-drastically-accelerate-progress-water-sanitation-and-hygiene-report. Accessed 10 April 2023.

USAID (-----); Power Africa in Nigeria. https://www.usaid.gov/powerafrica/nigeria. Accessed 15 April 2019.

VOA (2011); Corruption Puts Kenya's Educational Funding at Risk. http://m.voanews.com/158335.html. Accessed 29 August 2012.

White House (2009); Remarks by the President to Ghanaian Parliament. https://obamawhitehouse.archives.gov/the-press-office/remarks-president-ghanaian-parliament. Accessed July 2020.

WHO (2023); Global Health Workforce statistics database https://www.who.int/data/gho/data/themes/topics/health-workforce. Accessed 3 July 2023.

WHO (2016); Global Health Observatory (GHO) data. Retrieved from http://www.who.int/gho/child_health/mortality/mortality_under_five/en/.

World Bank (2011a); Leveraging Migration for Africa: Remittances, Skills, and Investments. https://documents1.worldbank.org/curated/en/721621468194077795/pdf/616360PUB0REPL0d0EPI009780821382578.pdf. Accessed 28 June 2023.

World Bank (2011b); Migration and Remittances Factbook 2011. https://doi.org/10.1596/978-0-8213-8218-9. Accessed 2 February 2019.

World Bank (2022); Literacy rate, adult total (% of people ages 15 and above). https://data.worldbank.org/indicator/SE.ADT.LITR.ZS. Accessed 19 July 2023.

Kolibri 360 GmbH
Ferdinand-Jühlke-Straße 7
99095 Erfurt, Deutschland
produktsicherheit@kolibri360.de